GREAT MARQUES
MERCEDES-BENZ

GREAT MARQUES
MERCEDES-BENZ

Roger Bell

Foreword by
Juan Manuel Fangio
General Editor
John Blunsden

OCTOPUS

Author's note

As a motoring journalist for 20 years, I must have written a few million words about cars, but this is my first book. So my thanks to John Blunsden for recommending me to Octopus, and secondly to Michael Gilliat, the publisher's senior editor of the series, for giving me the chance. To write the book it was necessary for me to raid the archives of *Motor*, where I worked for so long before Anthony Curtis took over the editor's hot seat, and those of former colleague Philip Turner. It was from their collections that I borrowed, among other reference works, Scott-Moncrieff's *Three-pointed Star*, revised by Peter Hull, which was an invaluable aid, as was Pomeroy's *Grand Prix Car* and Mercedes' own history book. My thanks, also, to Erik Johnson of Mercedes-Benz (UK) Ltd for all his time, assistance and recommendations, and to those members of the Mercedes-Benz club who provided either information or cars to photograph. I would also like to thank Rainer Schlegelmilch, Andrew Morland and Laurie Caddell who took the majority of the photographs, and the Daimler-Benz Museum in Germany for allowing our photographer access to the cars in their collection. Finally, I am most grateful to Juan Manuel Fangio for kindly providing the foreword to the book.
Roger Bell

ENDPAPERS, PAGES 1, 2–3, 4–5 The 1928 SSK with 225 bhp 7.1-litre blown engine.

PAGES 6/7 Juan Manuel Fangio in the W196 during the 1955 British Grand Prix at Aintree.

**First published in 1980 by
Octopus Books Limited,
59 Grosvenor Street,
London W1**

©1980 Octopus Books Limited

ISBN 0 7064 1371 7

Produced by Mandarin Publishers Limited,
22a Westlands Road, Quarry Bay,
Hong Kong

Printed in Hong Kong

Contents

Foreword by Juan Manuel Fangio

After reading these pages written by Roger Bell, about the evolution and development of the various car models produced by Daimler-Benz, I have to admit that I am overcome with nostalgia. To go through everything that is narrated here has been like living my life over again, with all those names paraded before me. It brings back the memory of scenes where I raced and won with the marque. It also draws me close to the racing companions of those unforgettable days.

This mood obliges me to make a confession. All racing drivers give themselves body and soul to the marque with which they race. But there always exists an opportunity for the spirit of the amateur to assert itself over the professional. This happened to me with Mercedes. It was like becoming a member of a family which had been waiting for me for a long time and with which I felt at home. I had every confidence racing under its emblem, and time has augmented this bond—today directed towards a business point of view, for at the present I sit on the Board of Directors of the Argentinian branch of the company—continuing a relationship which the years have only served to make greater still.

Juan Manuel Fangio

Juan Manuel Fangio
Buenos Aires

In the beginning...

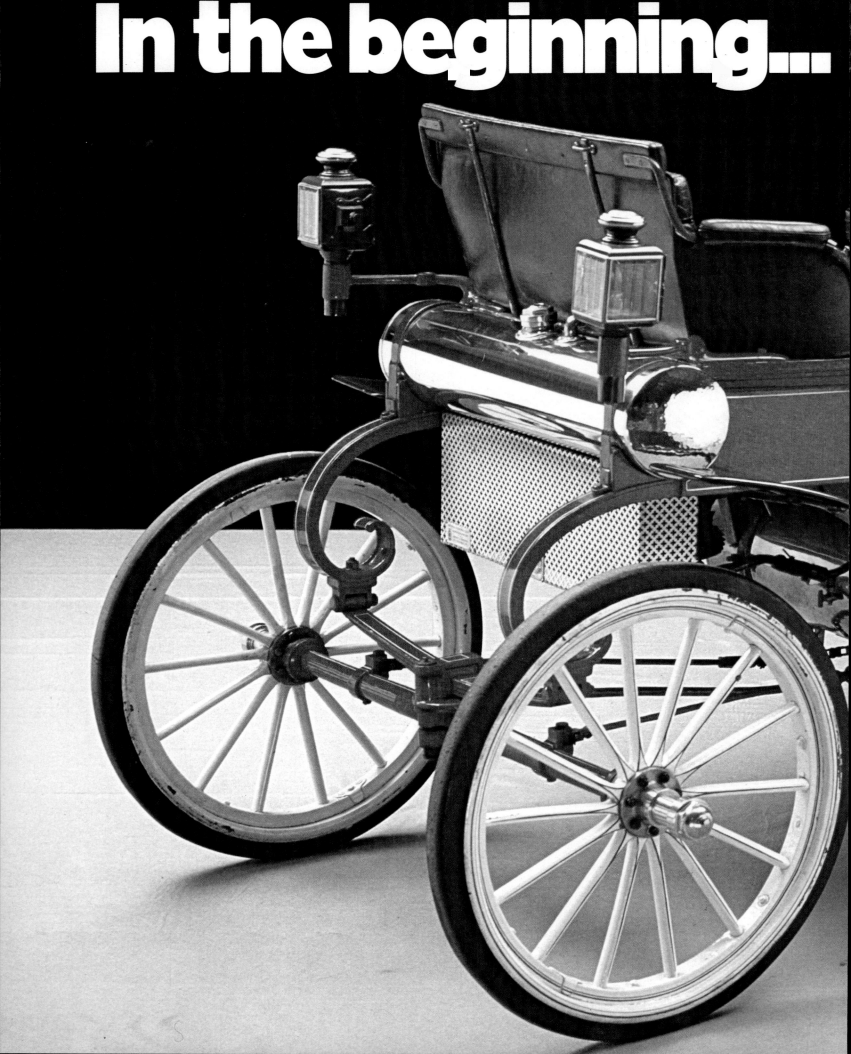

The three-pointed star of Mercedes-Benz is more than a symbol of prestige and success, more even than an epitaph to Gottlieb Daimler's dream of conquering travel on land, sea and air. Since this world-famous trademark was first embossed on the radiators of Mercedes cars in the early 1900s (it was not encircled by a ring and raised proudly above the bonnet until 1923) it has stood for the very finest in engineering and craftsmanship. Yet the origin of the name Mercedes which, as we shall see later, has nothing to do with the marque's founding fathers, does less than justice to the pioneers, Daimler and Karl Benz, the two geniuses whose early endeavours not only laid the foundation of the great Daimler-Benz empire that now bears their name, but also the modern automobile as we know it today.

The invention of the internal combustion engine

Neither Benz nor Daimler exactly invented the car. The first self-propelled vehicle, Joseph Cugnot's ungainly steam artillery carriage, had heaved itself along over a century before, and steam power had reached quite an advanced stage before more adventurous 19th-century engineers experimented with the internal combustion engine, which promised motive power without the encumbrance of a bulky boiler and external fire. The ingenious Frenchman Etienne Lenoir developed a highly successful gas engine but he failed to harness its power in a roadrunner. Nor did Marcus, Rivas, Edward Butler, Edouard Delamare-Deboutteville and others who made similar attempts. What sets Daimler and Benz apart from their contemporaries is that they succeeded where others had failed. What is more, they did so quite independently, neither man being remotely involved in the other's work. Indeed, they never even met, though their epoch-making experiments were conducted barely 60 miles apart in the Neckar valley in Germany. Daimler, 12 years older than Benz, died in 1900, over a quarter of a century before the concern he founded merged with that of his early rival. Karl Benz lived on not only to see the amalgamation of 1926, but to become an active part of it as a director. He died three years later in his eighties.

It was in 1886 that Daimler and Benz coincidentally produced a petrol-powered vehicle that actually worked, though they reached this common goal by very different routes.

Karl Benz

Benz, the son of a railway mechanic who died of pneumonia when young Karl was two, had a tough childhood and a determined mother who gave her bright son a sound education despite great financial hardship. Benz's interest in the newfangled gas engine, running on piped town gas and used for industrial power, was kindled by his tutor at the Karlsruhe Polytechnic, Ferdinand Redenbacher, and fanned by work on an early Lenoir 'gasmotor' in 1861. He graduated in 1864, worked briefly for a locksmith and then as a fitter in a locomotive works. The valuable experience he gained here served to underline his faith in the internal combustion engine: he saw little future in steam. After several more engineering jobs, the dedicated, hard-working Benz set up workshops to develop his own gas engine. The business floundered, but not before progress had been made on a two-stroke design with which he persevered despite the success of Dr Nikolaus Otto's patented four-stroke (hence the Otto cycle), the forerunner of modern car engines.

Following a dispute with business partners, he started afresh with funds from friends and established Benz & Co.: gas-engine manufacturers, though it was the application of the engine in a vehicle, rather than the motor itself, that obsessed Benz. By 1884 his high-speed two-stroke was running with advanced battery and trembler-coil ignition (the 'problem of all problems' he wrote later) rather than primitive hot-tube ignition used by Daimler and others. Benz turned to the four-stroke after the validity of the famous patent concerning Dr Nikolaus Otto's design had been questioned. And it was a four-stroke 'single' that powered the first Benz car, a three-wheeler tailor-made for the job rather than an adapted horse carriage.

To call Benz's first car a horseless carriage does less than justice to what was a primitive but remarkably well-conceived design. Remember, Benz had to start from scratch and work out for himself where to put the engine and how to transmit its puny 0.9 horsepower. The cumbersome single-cylinder engine, mounted behind a two-seater bench perched atop a flimsy chassis, had a huge horizontal flywheel to avoid any undesirable gyroscopic effects (good thinking but misguided as it happens), and drove the big-diameter wire-spoked rear wheels through a belt clutch to a remarkably advanced differential gear and then by chain from a

PAGES 8/9 *An 1894 Benz with face-to-face seats. The single-cylinder engine beneath the high rear seat drives through a two-speed transmission.*

BELOW LEFT *Benz's first four-wheeler was the primitive two-seater Victoria, shown here in its 1893 form. The big wooden-spoked rear wheels were driven by chains.*

RIGHT *Karl Benz, 1844–1929.*

BELOW *Benz's first car. Its horizontal engine, with water cooling and electric ignition, drove the wire-spoked wheels through a clever differential gear, belts and chains.*

countershaft. The water-cooled engine with its electric ignition and mechanically operated inlet valves, not to mention the clever differential, are all still with us on modern cars.

Benz's first tricycle (he failed at first to resolve the steering problem presented by a four-wheeler) achieved 12 km/h (7.5 mph) in 1886 and was in regular use in Mannheim the following year, much to the consternation of the police. The press loved his car but the authorities and other road users did not, not even after he had been awarded a Gold Medal at the Munich Exhibition in 1888. Bureaucracy bedevilled development and also deterred customers, which caused Benz's business partners to grow impatient and withdraw. Once more he had to start afresh—and again he was rescued from oblivion, financial support coming this time from two men of greater vision, one of whom, Julius Ganss, was a persuasive salesman who soon opened up new markets for the Benz three-wheelers. Meanwhile, the stationary petrol-engine business flourished, especially where there was no town gas laid on, allowing Benz—now in his forties—to concentrate on the development of his cars. He overcame the steering problem and built his first four-wheeler in 1892. His technical assistant August Horch was responsible for improving the performance of Benz's cars by increasing output by one horsepower,

though Benz himself was no speed enthusiast. In 1897 the first twin-cylinder engine was made, soon to power the famous 5 and 8 hp Benz models, and the cumbersome horizontal flywheel was abandoned. The wire wheels of his first tricycle were replaced by more conventional wood-spoke ones; Benz was, however, opposed to Michelin's early pneumatic tyres, introduced in 1896.

Despite important technical innovations, like the use of ball-bearing races in the back axle, not to mention quite a good range of cars, the conservative Benz, wedded to his own ideals, was slow to respond to advances elsewhere and was openly hostile to the quest for more power and speed. He stubbornly persevered with designs that were rapidly outmoded by those of rival manufacturers, resolutely sticking to his rear-mounted horizontally opposed twin-cylinder engine when in-line fours were all the rage. As early as 1891 Emile Levassor had evolved the successful driveline configuration of front engine, friction clutch, gearbox and final drive to the rear wheels: the Système Panhard as it was somewhat unfairly known. However, Benz was slow to adopt it, just as he was against the emergent sport of motor racing, particularly active in France, though he turned to it all the same in 1900. Benz had not taken kindly to his cars being known as 'Rogers', after his French representative Emile Roger who had raced Benz cars since 1894. Benz had some successes with his racers, including a class win in the famous London–Edinburgh–London 1000-mile trial in 1900, but they were not enough. Benz was losing ground and customers to more adventurous manufacturers, not least to the other father of the automobile, Gottlieb Daimler.

Gottlieb Daimler

Daimler was born in 1834, the second of four sons of a prosperous baker. As a boy, he shone at mathematics and geometry and was apprenticed to a gunsmith who developed young Gottlieb's innate creative gift. The pair of double-barrelled pistols he made, with carved walnut butts and chased barrels, are testimony to the skill and precision of his work. Nothing less than perfection was good enough for the diligent Daimler, who thrived on hard work and had no time for slackers. He left gunmaking to further his studies, won a scholarship, and in 1856 joined a locomotive works for a brief period.

Like Benz a little later, Daimler was not interested in steam and left to seek experience elsewhere. He spent two years in England (with Armstrong Whitworth and Roberts and Co.) and held other engineering positions in Germany before being appointed technical director of the Deutz works of Otto & Langen, makers of four-stroke gas engines. The relationship between Otto and Daimler was at best uneasy, but Daimler had a strong ally and lifelong friend in Wilhelm Maybach who was to play a leading role in the Daimler firm's fortunes later on. It was at Otto & Langen that Daimler instituted a quality-inspection system still used today.

The gas-engine business prospered but Daimler's relationship with Otto & Langen did not: he wanted to do more research and development, his employers were more concerned with production. Daimler was eased out. After a period in Russia in the oil business, he set up his own workshop in 1882 at Bad Cannstatt, first in a converted summerhouse, later in a small factory, and persuaded Maybach to join him. By 1883 they had perfected their hot-tube ignition, as far as the

LEFT *One of the first Benz cars to be fitted with a horizontally opposed twin-cylinder engine was this 1897 Dos-à-Dos.*

BELOW LEFT *Gottlieb Daimler's 1885 'single track' was the world's first motorcycle. It was powered by a 264 cc air-cooled engine.*

RIGHT *Two years after building their first truck, Gottlieb Daimler (right) and Wilhelm Maybach (second right) introduced this twin-cylinder five-tonner at the 1898 Paris show.*

BELOW *Daimler broke away from the 'horseless carriage' concept with this purpose-built wire-wheeled car in 1889.*

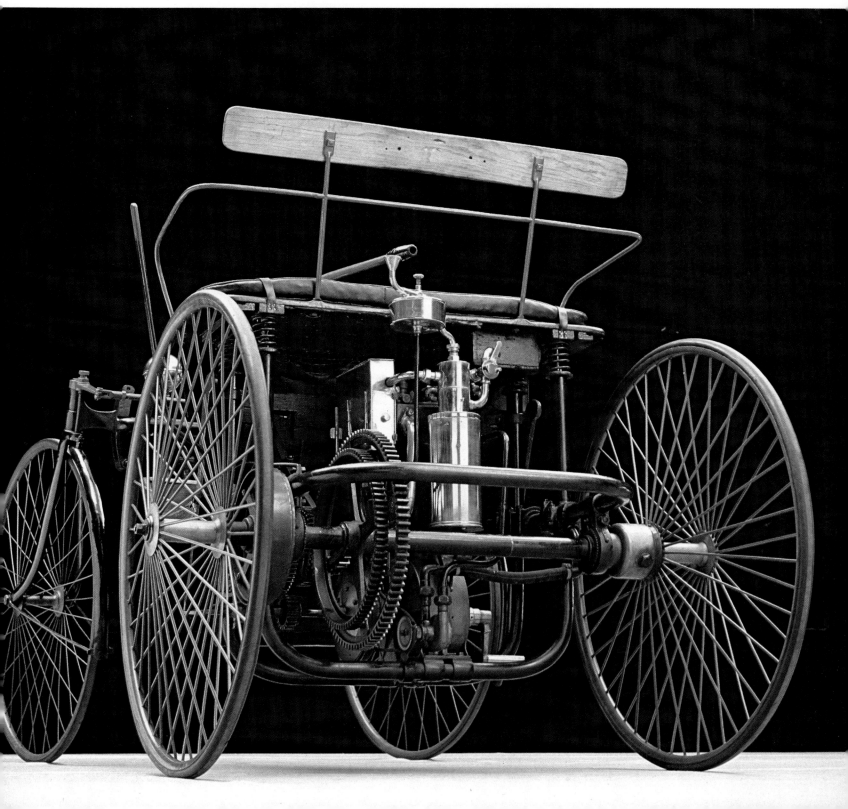

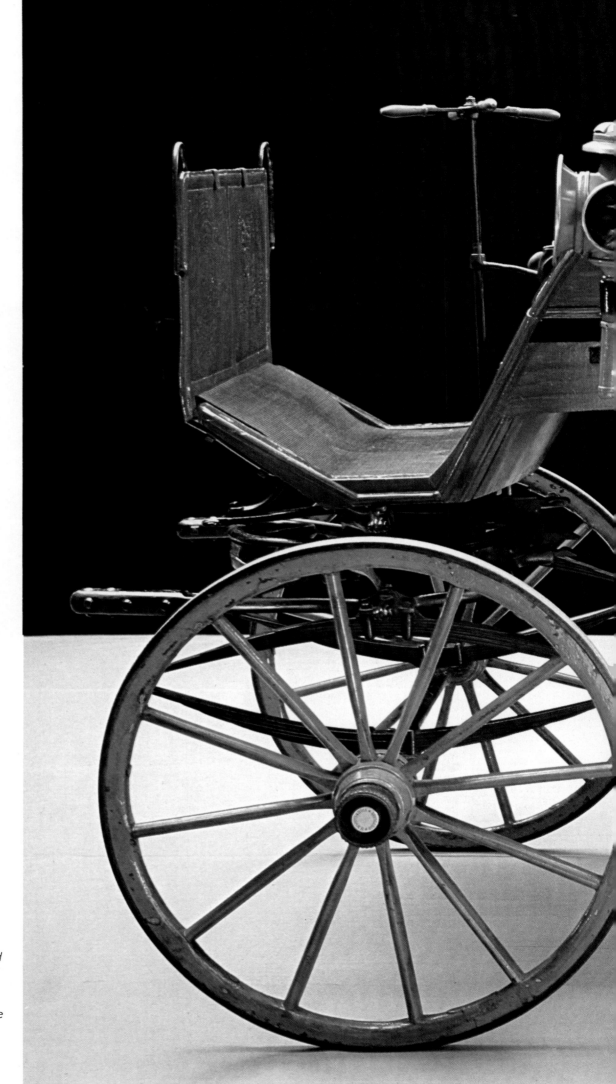

Gottlieb Daimler's first self-propelled four-wheeler was a converted carriage powered by a single-cylinder water-cooled engine. Belts and pulleys conveyed the drive to pinions that engaged with cogs on the back wheels. To steer, the whole of the front axle was turned by the handlebars. The vehicle first ran in 1886, the same year as Benz's three-wheeler.

14

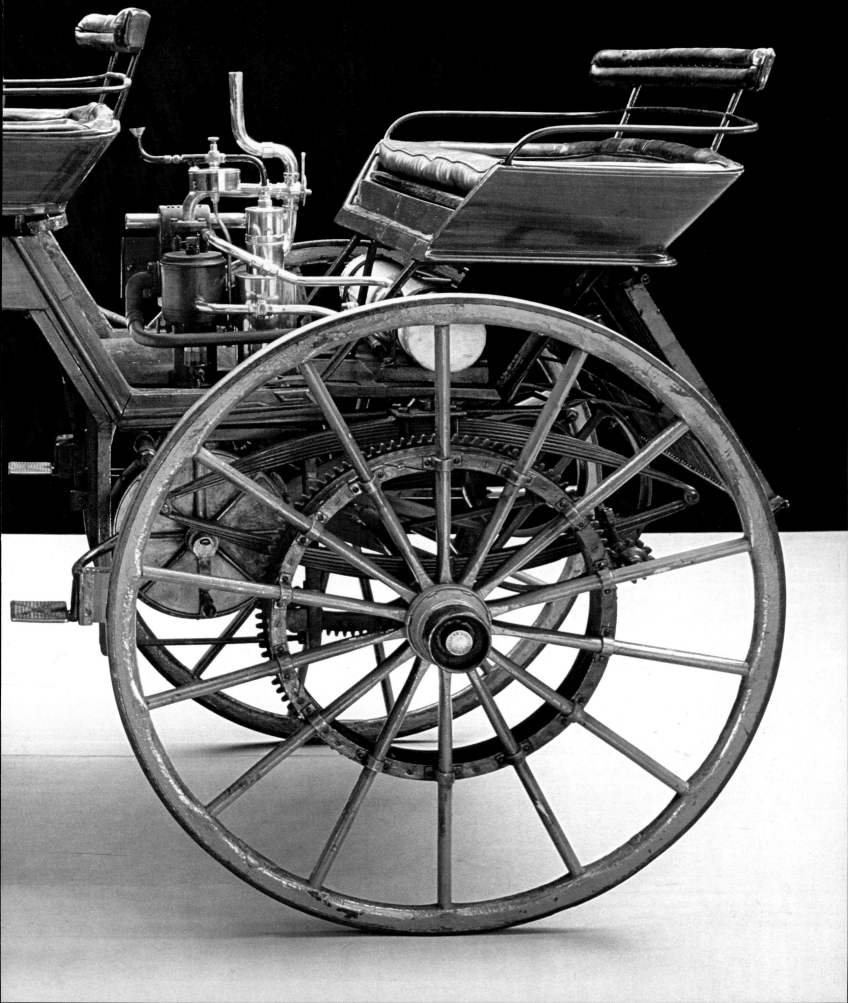

intrinsic shortcomings of so crude an arrangement would allow. Nevertheless, by using its own tanked fuel (benzine or petrol, obtained from chemists in those days) Daimler's single-cylinder engine was the first to run without piped mains gas. Moreover, it ran at unheard-of speeds of up to 900 rpm. Instead of an external flame that had to be 'charged' into the compressed cylinder gases to induce combustion, Daimler used a sealed tube with the open end protruding into the cylinder head and the closed one heated by an outside petrol-burning bunsen. The gases ignited spontaneously as they were forced into the red-hot tube. Engine speed was governed by control of exhaust valve lift. Two years later, Daimler was producing even more advanced vertical engines, the crankshaft and small flywheel of which were enclosed in an oil housing.

Unlike Benz, Daimler was not obsessed solely with the automobile. His vision was to provide powered transport for everyone and everything, on land, sea and air. His first self-propelled vehicle, built in 1885, was a motorcycle, or 'single track' as it was then known. This ungainly wood-and-iron contraption, powered by an air-cooled ½ bhp engine, was successfully ridden by Daimler's eldest son Paul, but the patented design was not developed. His first powered boat, which so impressed Prince Bismarck that he later bought one, led to a flourishing marine division. In 1886, while Benz was completing his three-wheeler, Daimler installed one of his more powerful engines in a converted horse-drawn carriage to produce the world's first successful four-wheel car. Its 1½ bhp water-cooled engine drove through a system of belts, pulleys and a simple slip-disc differential to pinions that engaged with large toothed rims attached to the rear wheels. It was crude but it worked. So, too, did the tram he built for the local Cannstatt authorities, and the taxi that went into service at Stuttgart station in 1888. Daimler engines were soon powering fire engines, timber saws and the world's first dirigible, built with balloonist Dr Karl Wolfert. The single-cylinder 2 bhp engine could not cope with the corpulent doctor's weight so a young spectator was recruited to fly the craft. History does not record the name of the first powered-flight pilot.

Daimler's third car was a specially made four-wheeler, the tubular frame of which acted as the radiator for the rear-mounted V-twin engine's cooling water. A cone clutch transmitted the 1½ bhp through a four-speed gearbox and the wire-spoked front wheels were carried by cycle-type forks with proper steering geometry, although it was tiller operated. Impressed by the car's performance, Peugeot and Panhard et Levassor in France switched to Daimler engines in the early 1890s, which had a big influence on the French motor industry, soon to outstrip that of Germany. In the 1894 Paris–Rouen trials, Daimler-powered Peugeots were second, third and fifth (beaten by Count Albert de Dion's steamer), and Emile Levassor won the 1895 Paris–Bordeaux–Paris race in a Panhard-Daimler, covering the 1199 km (745 miles) in under 49 hours single-handed. This epic feat underlined the superiority of Franco-German machines.

By then, four-cylinder 10 bhp Daimler engines were successfully powering railcars, and in 1892 came the first vertical twin, later to oust the V-twin, with improved valve gear and speed control. The engine business flourished, but after a dispute with his co-directors, Daimler and Maybach cut themselves adrift from the company in 1892 and returned to more research and development, which resulted in Maybach's jet carburettor and patented belt-drive car. Three years later, the two engineers returned to a reconstituted Daimler Motoren-Gesellschaft with a strong new programme for car production.

The Mercedes name

Daimler was by now a sick man but before his death in 1900 he saw several important developments: the adoption of low-tension magneto ignition instead of hot-tube after Robert Bosch had solved the problem of accurate spark control; the use of pneumatic tyres on the front-engined Phœnix, Victoria, Phaeton and Vis-à-Vis (face-to-face) models; a return to dirigible propulsion, which ended tragically with a fatal accident to Dr Wolfert, though not before attracting the attention of Count Zeppelin; and, in 1896, a four-cylinder 6 hp speedster in response to an enquiry from the rich and influential Austrian banker, businessman and diplomat, Emile Jellinek (pronounced Yellinek). This adapted 6 hp Phaeton, which Daimler did not really approve of, handled well and did 42 km/h (26 mph)—but it was not fast enough to beat the speed-crazy French. The upright, short-wheelbase Daimler Phœnix 23 hp racer of 1899 was not the final answer either, and when works driver Wilhelm Bauer was killed while competing in one of these hard-to-handle cars on the La Turbie hill climb, the Cannstatt works withdrew from the competition. But not for long. Consul-General Jellinek, who was a Daimler enthusiast as well as a distributor (a director and backer too later on), was not deterred. He

16

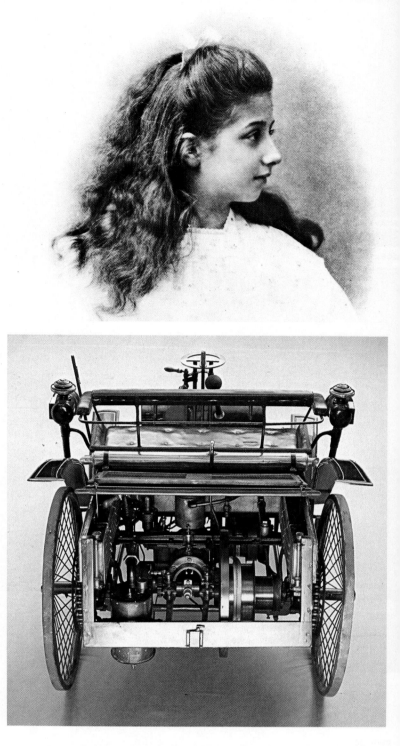

TOP *Emile Jellinek's beautiful daughter, Mercédès, whose name was adopted for all Daimler's cars from 1901 after her wealthy, influential father had inspired a new all-conquering racer.*

ABOVE *The working end of Daimler's 1893 belt-drive car which incorporated several patents granted the previous year.*

RIGHT *Driver outside, passengers within. This closed Daimler of the mid-1890s still had twist-axle steering and a rear-mounted engine driving wood-spoke wheels by exposed chains.*

advocated something even more powerful with a longer wheelbase and a lower centre of gravity. What is more, he pledged to buy 36 such cars in return for the selling rights in Austria, Belgium, Hungary, America and France, provided he could name the cars after his daughter, Mercédès—the name under which he had previously raced Daimler cars.

It was not uncommon for the gentry of the period to use such pseudonyms, often to avoid conflict with a disapproving family for social or safety reasons. Jellinek may well have originally chosen the name lightheartedly on the spur of the moment out of nothing more than sentiment. If so, it was a momentous whim. Although the name is of Spanish origin (like Jellinek's wife) it *sounded* French, which suited the enterprising businessman's activities in France, even though it led to contractual problems—resolved in Jellinek's favour—with Panhard et

Levassor, who were still building Daimler engines under licence. Whether Gottlieb Daimler, by now a very sick man, approved of Jellinek's proposals is uncertain, but Maybach and his co-directors did and the deal went through.

The Daimler 35 hp: the first Mercedes

It is thought that Maybach based his design for Jellinek's racer on that of Paul Daimler's small twin-cylinder car of 1899 which, among several advanced features, had a honeycomb radiator, an integral crankcase/gearbox, column-mounted gear lever and a foot-operated throttle. The new 35 hp four-cylinder car was a sensation, and immediately outdated everything else on the roads. The 5.9-litre engine was relatively small compared with that of some rival monsters, but very powerful for its size and weight. Its mechanically operated inlet valves ensured good filling of the T-shaped combustion chambers through two carburettors, one for each pair of cast cylinders with integral heads. The Bosch low-tension magneto ignition could be advanced and retarded as required, and the large honeycomb radiator cooled the small volume of water that was pumped round the engine. A coil-spring clutch transmitted the 35 bhp, developed at 1000 rpm, through a four-speed gearbox operated by a gate change, to a countershaft that drove the rear wheels by sprockets and chains. Deep-section chassis pressings gave greater strength and rigidity than on previous cars, resulting in better roadholding and handling.

The new model, which doubled as racer and tourer, dominated the Nice Week competitions held in the south of France in March 1901, reaching speeds of 85 km/h (53 mph). Its rakish appearance and amazing performance abruptly ended the era of the horseless carriage: real automobiles arrived with the first Mercédès (the accents were later dropped), which made such an impact that the name was thereafter adopted by the Daimler company for all its cars. Thus did Emile Jellinek's daughter become part of motoring history, though the good lady herself probably enjoyed a less fortunate life than the car named after her. Following two allegedly unhappy marriages she died, as Baroness Weigel, in 1929, three years after the Daimler and Benz amalgamation.

So, the turn of the century saw Daimler's Mercedes cars setting the pace in both engineering and competition under the brilliant Wilhelm Maybach. Meanwhile, not far down the road, the fortunes of the conservative Benz were at a lower ebb, though they were not to stay that way for long.

Mercedes
v.
Benz

Gottlieb Daimler's death, said to have been caused by overwork, at the age of 66 left the Daimler Motoren-Gesellschaft under the control of financier Max Duttenhofer; Daimler's sons Paul and Adolf, later to become directors, at this stage played no more than supporting roles to Wilhelm Maybach, generally recognized as the most talented automobile designer of his day.

Following unexpected defeat in the prestigious Paris–Berlin race of 1902, in which works driver Wilhelm Werner could manage no better than 14th place in a 35 hp Mercedes behind the winning 60 hp Mors, Maybach produced a much-improved 40 hp car which, as its predecessor had done the previous year, dominated the 1902 Nice Week. Built to the new 1000 kg (2205 lb) formula, the cars were lighter and more powerful than before, with remarkably quiet and flexible four-cylinder engines. Advanced carburation and mechanical inlet valves ensured excellent induction, combustion and control throughout the effective 200–1200 rpm rev range. All the car's moving parts except those of the engine ran on ball bearings, and the wheels were carried by weldless drawn-steel tube axles—later replaced by wrought-iron I-section ones—attached to a channel-section steel chassis. The four-speed gearbox was combined in one unit with the differential and final drive chain-and-sprocket countershaft. Known as the Mercedes-Simplex, these 40 hp racers were supported by a range of touring cars of similar concept: the 12/16, 18/22, 28/32 and 40/45. The first figure in this confusing model nomenclature, which many manufacturers used, denotes the taxable horsepower, the second the effective output. As the racing cars were not licensed, they were known only by the latter, more meaningful figure, which between 1901 and 1907 increased from 35 to 120 bhp.

Again, Mercedes dominated Nice Week in 1903, this time with the 60 hp racer with even lighter, stronger stamped U-shaped frame members and the bore and stroke dimensions of the engine increased to 170 × 140 mm. One of these cars covered the flying mile at Nice at 119.6 km/h (74.3 mph). Soon after came the mighty 90 hp, which made its debut in the ill-fated Paris–Madrid marathon of 1903. Competition among the leading manufacturers of France, Germany, Italy and Britain was by now intense and many of the 112 'heavies' running in the 1000 kg category had more power than their extensively drilled and lightened chassis could handle. Their roadholding on skinny, puncture-prone tyres was poor, their brakes even worse. After a series of terrible accidents, in which many spectators were killed or maimed, the French authorities stopped the race at Bordeaux, and Fernand Gabriel, leading at the time on his Mors, was declared the winner. It was the last of the epic city-to-city races. With their demise the Gordon Bennett Trophy—instigated in 1899 by James Gordon Bennett, proprietor of the *New York Times*, to stimulate interest in international motor racing—assumed a new importance. S.F. Edge in a Napier had unexpectedly won the 1902 event and as the rules decreed that the race was to be held in the country of the previous year's winner, the 1903 Gordon Bennett Trophy should have taken place in England. However, a government ban forced the organizers to stage the race in Ireland instead. Unfortunately all five of the 90 hp Mercedes that

Daimler had built for the Trophy were destroyed by fire, along with many production cars and much of the Cannstatt works. But it made no difference to the outcome. The bearded Belgian tyre maker, Camille Jenatzy, survivor of many horrific crashes and daredevil of the Mercedes team, won in a borrowed 60 hp car, despite strong opposition from Napier, Panhard, Mors, Peerless and others. It was a great victory that underlined the superiority of the big Mercedes racers, especially the legendary 60 hp, which had become the standard by which all others were judged.

The death of Duttenhofer and the disastrous fire that virtually destroyed the Cannstatt factory marred an otherwise successful year for Mercedes in 1903. But the company recovered quickly from these setbacks and, although Mercedes scored no outright wins during Nice Week, competition success continued both in Europe and America, W.K. Vanderbilt Jun. setting several US records in a 90 hp.

As Germany had fielded the winning Gordon Bennett car the previous year, the Mercedes were on home ground for the 1904 race, to be run over four laps of an 140 km (87-mile) circuit around Homburg. The official German entry consisted of two 90 hp Mercedes and Fritz von Opel (founder of Opel cars) in an Opel-Darracq but three Austrian-entered 90s effectively gave Mercedes a five-car team to pit against powerful British, French and Italian entries. The Germans were hot favourites but, although Jenatzy's 90 hp was always in with a chance, he could not match the remarkable pace of Léon Théry's lone French Richard Brasier, which won by 11 minutes.

So the Gordon Bennett Trophy, the most coveted prize in motor racing at the time, returned to France from whence Edge had wrested it two years earlier. Théry's victory not only put the name of Brasier firmly on the map, but also changed the course of motor racing. France, dissatisfied with the Gordon Bennett rules—as the world's leading car manufacturers the French felt they should be allowed to field more than three cars—ran the 1905 race under protest, though again it was Théry on his Brasier who won despite intense competition from the new Maybach-designed 120 hp Mercedes. Jenatzy had started as favourite but the feeble tyres could not handle the car's great power and he was never in the running. The French were now in a predicament. They had sworn to boycott any future Gordon Bennett race yet, as winners, they were due to host it again in 1906. An international showdown was avoided when alternative proposals for the first French Grand Prix, forerunner of today's Formula 1 GPs, were accepted instead. The Gordon Bennett's 1000 kg weight limit was retained, but there was no restriction on the number of cars any one country could enter. Moreover, all running repairs had to be done by the driver and his riding mechanic.

The French Grand Prix was the big event of 1906 and, although the Mercedes cars acquitted themselves well against stiff opposition from Fiat, Hotchkiss, Panhard, Darracq, Gobron-Brillié and others, it was a French Renault that won.

By now Maybach had replaced low-tension ignition with the high-tension magneto system developed by Robert Bosch, founder of the

PAGES 18/19 *This splendid 1912 20 hp Benz, fitted with four-seater open tourer body, had a four-cylinder engine and a conventional driveline. Success in the Prince Henry Trials underlined Benz's sporting reputation.*

LEFT *A 1902 Mercedes 25/28, with four-cylinder engine and chain drive, evolved from the revolutionary 35 hp car that was inspired by Jellinek and designed by Maybach two years before.*

ABOVE RIGHT *Benz racing cars began making their mark in international racing in 1908 when Victor Hémery won the St Petersburg to Moscow event and works engineer Fritz Erle, shown here, won the Prince Henry Trials. Poor roads and feeble tyres made the going very tough.*

electrical business empire that still bears his name. Maybach also produced his first six-cylinder racer which was fast but, by Mercedes high standards, also reputedly rather troublesome. A refined 70 hp road car soon followed. The six big cylinders, cast in pairs, had bore and stroke dimensions of 120 × 140 mm, and were fed by side valves operated by gear-driven camshafts on each side of the block. The drive was through a four-speed gearbox and shaft to bevel gears on the live back axle: a design adopted in 1908 for all but the most powerful of Daimler's cars, which retained sprockets and chains.

For Mercedes 1907 was a poor year. Privateers scored their customary wins at Daytona—Steinway, the piano manufacturer, was by now marketing Mercedes-built chassis with American coachwork and accessories in the United States—and the first race at Brooklands, in July 1907, was won by J.E. Hutton, the British Mercedes agent, in a 120 hp car. But there were no major victories for Daimler. What is more, dwindling sales forced the company to cut its labour force by almost a half during the slump of 1907–8, and the influential sales supremo Emile Jellinek retired from the board through ill health. An even bigger loss, though, was that of Wilhelm Maybach who left at the age of 61 to start what became a very successful business of his own. Maybach's engines were later to power Count Zeppelin's dirigibles, and even exotic and exclusive cars bearing his own name. But Maybach is best remembered for his years at Daimler where he had a profound influence on the design and development of the automobile during that revolutionary period at the turn of the century.

Not that Daimler's activities were confined to cars: the company was by 1907 firmly established in the truck, bus, marine and stationary engine fields, with manufacturing plants in Berlin and Austria (run for a time by Paul Daimler) as well as Bad Cannstatt.

The Benz Parsifal and the early touring cars and racers

In the early 1900s Daimler's great Mercedes racers overshadowed the activities of Karl Benz, whose modest cars of outmoded design were better known for their reliability and comfort than for speed. Not that they had been commercially unsuccessful: the Velo and Comfortable were among the best-selling models of their time and as a volume producer, Benz was in the big league in 1899 with agencies throughout the world. But Benz was not a racing man and sales of his outdated cars began to fall sharply in the early 1900s. Even then it was co-director Julius Ganss rather than the conservative Benz who forced a change of direction with a front-engined, shaft-driven car based on a Renault design. For a time this completely new Benz, called the Parsifal, was built alongside the old-fashioned cars by French fitters under the direction of Marius Barbarou. However, the Parsifal, in its original two-cylinder form, was underpowered and a commercial failure. The company's fortunes went from bad to worse and Karl Benz and his son Eugen resigned after a boardroom dispute. Ganss had been on the right track but with the company now well in the red, he too was compelled to resign.

Karl Benz's period of exile was brief. He returned to the board,

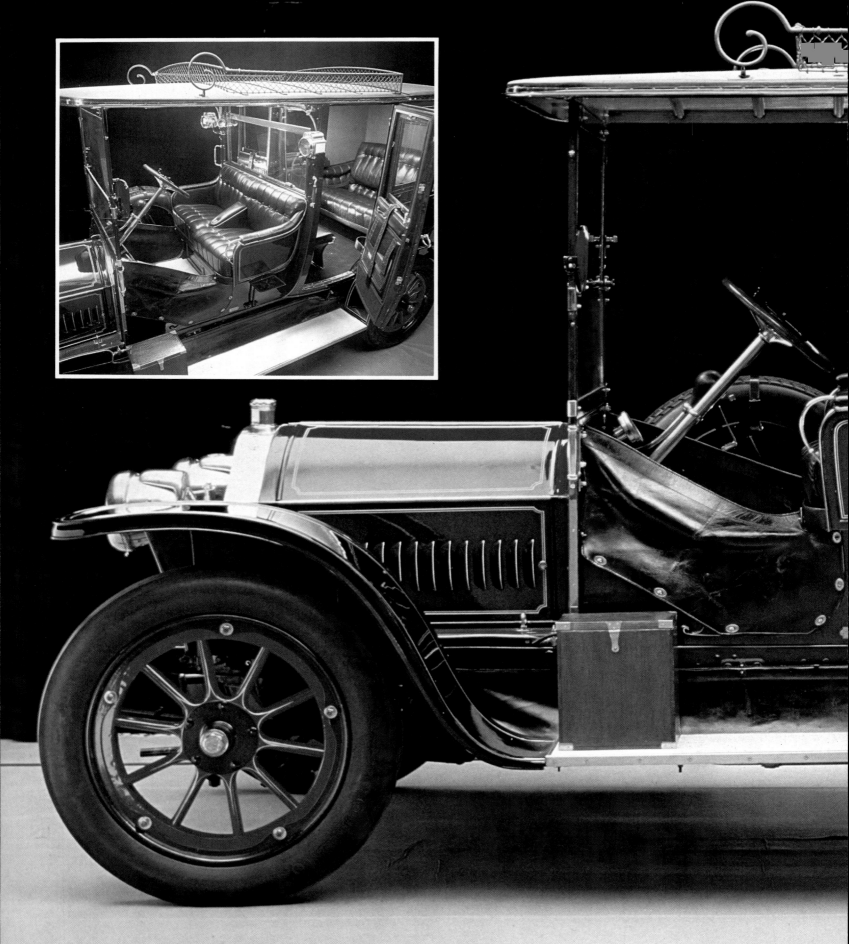

reworked the Parsifal's chassis and replaced its two-cylinder engine with a new in-line four-cylinder of advanced design with mechanically operated inlet and exhaust valves: something of a novelty as many cars still employed automatic inlet valves opened by suction. They were operated by camshafts, one each side of the two siamesed blocks, driven from the crankshaft by spur gears. With this car the company revolutionized the Benz model range and image virtually overnight. Out went the old flat-twin, belt-drive 8/10, 10/12 and 12/14 runabouts to be replaced with a powerful 28 hp modern car that had up-to-the-minute shaft drive. It was a

This 1909 Benz limousine 20/35 was among the leaders of its day in luxury motoring. The figures in the nomenclature indicate respectively the taxable horsepower in Germany and the actual output of the four-cylinder engine. INSET *The lavishly appointed interior.*

massive step forward that immediately changed Benz's fortunes. Even more powerful 40 and 60 hp cars soon followed and by 1904 Benz had a range of touring cars to match that of Mercedes. Both manufacturers included in their range quality cars of modest size and power but they

concentrated on the large, exclusive market; Benz went as far as to list in a 1905 advertisement all the company's royal and titled customers. Prince Henry of Prussia was a loyal Benz supporter and the elegant 60 hp Double Phaeton built for him caused a sensation at the 1906 Berlin exhibition.

Although Benz did well in the Herkomer Trophy, a prestige event instigated by the portrait painter Hubert von Herkomer for touring cars rather than racers—a 40 hp car won in 1906 and a 50 hp took the third and last Herkomer of 1907—it was not until 1907/8 that Benz racing cars really made their mark in international racing. In 1908 works engineer/

driver Fritz Erle won the Prince Henry Trials and the great Victor Hémery, recruited from France into the Benz team, won the 690 km (429-mile) St Petersburg to Moscow race from Darracq and Itala first time out in Hans Nibel's new 161 km/h (100 mph) 120 hp Benz, averaging over 80 km/h (50 mph) on appalling roads.

Nibel became to Benz what Maybach had been to Daimler and as chief engineer he headed the company's design team for the next 20 years. Under a new formula that limited the bore of four-cylinder engines to 155 mm, Benz produced a long (200 mm) stroke engine of 15,095 cc that

23

developed 150 bhp. Its cylinders were cast in pairs and the overhead valves were operated by an enclosed camshaft by pushrods and rockers. Two sparking plugs per cylinder ensured efficient combustion of mixture from Benz's rotary slide-valve carburettor with its variable jet. The chassis was based on that of the high-class tourers, except that the final drive was by sprockets and chains rather than by shaft to a crown wheel and pinion. Braking was by rear drums and bands on the drive shafts.

It was in one of these cars that Hémery finished second to Christian Lautenschlager's Mercedes in the 1908 French Grand Prix, with another Benz third, making it a resounding clean sweep for the Germans. This was the last great Mercedes victory for some years, however, because Daimler thereafter withdrew from racing because of the enormous costs. Several other manufacturers pulled out at the same time as a result of an international pact to abstain from the big events. Not so Benz who, far from cutting back, committed even bigger sums of money to the company racing programme.

The legendary Blitzen Benz

The 150 hp car captured several records in America, the great Barney Oldfield taking the standing-start mile at Indianapolis in 43.1 seconds. But it was Nibel's incredible 200 hp Blitzen ('Lightning') Benz with its thin, torpedo-like body that stole the limelight from 1909 on, taking several new world speed records. It achieved a remarkable 205 km/h (127.4 mph) at Brooklands in 1909, 210.9 km/h (131.1 mph) at Daytona in 1910, and a resounding 228 km/h (141.7 mph) there the following year. In fact this legendary Benz held the world speed record for 15 years from 1909 to 1924. Increasing the bore of the big four-cylinder engine to 185 mm (the 200 mm stroke was retained) took the capacity to 21.5 litres and in the highest of its four ratios the car was geared to do 225 km/h (140 mph) at an engine speed of 1400 rpm—little more than a tickover speed for a modern engine. Even the great Jenatzy, driving an elderly 180 hp Mercedes, was no match for Erle's Blitzen Benz at the Gaillon hill climb in France in 1911. Shortly after this, the red-bearded Belgian ace, who had scored so many fine victories for Mercedes, retired from serious racing. Erle, too, retired the following year after averaging a record 162.5 km/h (101 mph) up the famous French hill in a two-seater Blitzen.

These and other competition successes, including a first and second in the 1910 American Grand Prix, certainly stimulated sales of Benz's rather dull but well-engineered and elegant road cars, especially while the rival Daimlers were away from racing. They were not all expensive, exclusive models, either. The engine of the 14/30 introduced in 1909 had a one-piece cylinder block with a bore and stroke of 90 × 140 mm and an offset crankshaft so that the camshaft could be placed near the centre of the block. In 1911 Benz introduced a silent chain camshaft drive on the smallest 8/18 model, as well as pressurized lubrication. This car, which cost £365 in Britain, was described by *The Autocar* as 'a full-sized touring car in miniature'. The magazine praised its quiet and flexible four-cylinder engine with its self-advancing Eisemann magneto ignition, its comfortable ride, easy gear change and strong brakes. Also offered in the Benz range at this time were the 15/25, 28/35, 38/45, 45/65 and 45/90, all with four-cylinder engines. The Prince Henry trials had led to the introduction of a range of sports cars too.

The Daimler range and the three-pointed star

Although Daimler had withdrawn from racing in 1908, the company was very active in other spheres. Paul Daimler took over as chief engineer when Maybach retired (later on, in 1913, he also assumed the responsibility of technical director when his brother Adolf died at the age of 42). From 1908 to 1913 Daimler built up an extensive range of shaft-drive cars—the 18/18, 10/20, 14/35, 21/35, 22/40 and 28/60—though chains were still used to drive the more powerful models. Daimler also introduced a new range of engines with overhead inlet valves and side exhausts to improve breathing, piston-type carburettors with preheating, high-tension ignition and a plunger oil pump, driven by the water-pump shaft to force-feed all the engine bearings.

It was in 1909 that the three-pointed star was adopted as Daimler's trademark. The story goes that Gottlieb Daimler had once told his young sons of a star that would rise from the family home to bring happiness and

The legendary Blitzen (Lightning) Benz. This famous racing car, designed by Hans Nibel, won many events and captured numerous records. It lapped Brooklands at 205 km/h (127.4 mph) in 1909 and held the land speed record at 228 km/h (141.7 mph) for several years. INSET *The huge four-cylinder engine had a capacity of 21.5 litres in its largest form.*

fortune. It was a tale that caught the imagination of the Daimler board who adopted the star as a tribute to the company's founder, though not without some difficulty as many other firms had already registered a trademark of similar design. At first, both three- and four-pointed stars were registered, but it was only the now world-famous three-pronged emblem that was thereafter embossed on to the already distinctive pointed radiators of Mercedes cars.

In the quest for quietness and refinement, Daimler introduced a series of sleeve-valve engines in 1909, built under licence from the American Charles Knight. Instead of using noisy poppet valve gear, induction and exhaust was by means of ported cylindrical 'sleeves' that slithered between pistons and cylinders, giving not only quieter running but, claimed Daimler, more power in the 500–1500 rpm range. Efficient lubrication of the sleeves was all important, but Daimler resolved the problem and continued to manufacture Knight-engined cars, including the 10/60, 16/40, 16/45 and 16/50 models, until 1923. Sleeve-valve engines also powered some successful competition cars, including Ralph Mulford's fifth-placed racer in the 1913 Indianapolis 500.

By 1912, Daimler's range of cars extended from the little 10/25 two-seater (costing £420 in Britain) to the great 37/90 luxury tourer, with

1914 GRAND PRIX MERCEDES	
ENGINE	
Cylinders	4 in line separately forged steel barrels, water cooled
Bore/stroke mm	93 × 165
Capacity cc	4483
Valves	4 per cylinder operated by single overhead camshaft
Carburation	Single Mercedes
Ignition	Two Bosch high-tension magnetos firing 12 plugs – three per cylinder
Power	115 bhp at 3200 rpm
DRIVE TRAIN	
Clutch	Double cone, mechanically operated
Gearbox	4-speed with changeable ratios, separate from engine
Drive	Torque-tube to crown and pinion for each halfshaft with common differential
CHASSIS	
Frame	Channel section steel
Front suspension	Live axle on semi-elliptic leaf springs
Rear suspension	Live axle on semi-elliptic leaf springs
Steering	Worm and nut, 1½ turns lock to lock
Brakes	Mercedes expanding shoe rear drums, mechanically operated
Wheels	Rudge Whitworth detachable, wire-spoke
Weight	1093 kg (2410 lb)
PERFORMANCE	
Max speed	180 km/h (112 mph)

ABOVE *Lautenschlager winning the 1914 French Grand Prix. The meticulously prepared Mercedes team, which had practised on the course for weeks before the race, finished first, second and third after outpacing a 47-car field that included Delages and Peugeots.* TOP LEFT *A wheel change for Louis Wagner who finished second.*

LEFT *Sleeve-valve engines of various sizes, made under licence from the American Charles Knight, were produced by Mercedes from 1910 to 1924. This is a 1910–13 open tourer.*

coachwork to choice. All had four-cylinder engines, some with sleeve valves, others with poppets, though only the larger, more powerful cars retained chain drive. Maybach's first and only six-cylinder Mercedes—the racer and two tourers—lasted for only a brief period, from 1906 to 1907, but a new 28/95 luxury six, again short-lived, was introduced in 1914.

Although Daimler was absent from the racing tracks from 1908 to 1913, Mercedes cars remained very competitive and put up some notable performances. Driving a 1908 car, Ralph DePalma finished third at Indianapolis in 1911, and was leading the 1912 race before his engine failed. Later that year, he won the Vanderbilt Cup in the same car. The great Mercedes comeback was in 1914, but Daimler actually returned to racing in 1913 with a four-car team for the French Grand Prix held at Le Mans. Two of the Daimler cars were much-modified 1908 racers, but the other two were new chain-driven machines powered experimentally by small six-cylinder aero engines with a single overhead camshaft operating two inclined valves per cylinder. In this respect, they were already outdated by the remarkable Henry-designed Peugeot, winner of the 1912 French Grand Prix, which boasted twin overhead camshafts operating four valves per cylinder. Peugeot did not contest the 1913 race, which was won by Paul Bablot's Delage, but a Henry Peugeot won the Coupe de l'Auto at Boulogne later the same year.

A practised victory, 1914

With the stormclouds of war gathering over Europe, the 1914 French Grand Prix became more than just another motor race. It was a battle for national pride and prestige. Six countries and many more manufacturers were represented by 47 cars, running to a 4.5-litre engine capacity limit thought to favour the all-conquering Delages and Peugeots, led by French idols Georges Boillot and Jules Goux, especially as they had four-wheel brakes like the Italian Fiats. The British Sunbeams, too, were in with a good chance and there were also strong entries from Vauxhall, Opel, and others. But it was the five-car team of Mercedes that most mystified and worried the French. For months before the race the Germans were to be seen practising on each and every part of the 38 km (23½-mile) triangular course near Lyons, changing this, modifying that, until they had got everything right. The four-cylinder long-stroke Daimler engines, now with four valves per cylinder operated from a single overhead camshaft, developed 115 bhp at 3200 rpm—a very high speed for those days. What is more, the engines, with their steel cylinders surrounded by welded-sheet water jackets, could sustain high revolutions for long periods.

The cars started two at a time at half-minute intervals, with 20 laps, over 750 km (466 miles) ahead of them. By the end of the first lap it was evident that the new Mercedes, even without front-wheel brakes, said to be worth a minute a lap, were the fastest cars. Max Sailer's white machine led Boillot's blue Peugeot by an ever-increasing margin until the engine of the leading Mercedes 'hare', intended to stretch the opposition, failed. Strictly to order, Lautenschlager, Louis Wagner (who was French) and Otto Salzer then moved up, Lautenschlager, winner of the 1908 French GP, taking the lead from Boillot on the 18th lap and pulling away comfortably. The Peugeot, now harassed by Wagner for second place, failed on the 19th lap, giving the German cars a sweeping one-two-three finish in front of a stunned and stonily silent French crowd. Soon after, France and Germany were at war.

Amalgamation

Although her factories were not destroyed by air attacks as they were to be later in World War 2, the Kaiser's defeated Germany was in financial ruin after the 1914–18 conflagration. The home market was hardly big enough to support one manufacturer, let alone the 86 that existed in Germany at the time. In the wildest period of inflation and devaluation the world has ever seen, many car makers inevitably went to the wall, speeded to bankruptcy by competition from abroad when protective imports tariffs were lowered to suit the government's fiscal policies. Deprived of essential raw materials, many manufacturers lowered their standards in the fight for survival and turned out cheap, shoddy goods for a market that could afford little better.

Such a course was not open to the great Daimler and Benz concerns. From humble beginnings, both had developed into industrial giants whose worldwide reputations were founded on engineering quality of the highest standards. Daimler, which had its roots in the summerhouse of a modest villa at Bad Cannstatt (now a memorial to Gottlieb Daimler) had soon outgrown the original works established in 1890. The fire that largely destroyed them in 1903 hastened the move to the much bigger Untertürkheim factory which was in operation by 1904. Daimler's Sindelfingen works near Stuttgart were established during World War 1 for aero-engine manufacture—aircraft too a little later—and there were plants elsewhere, including the Austro-Daimler factory in Austria.

Benz's tremendous pre-war expansion was concentrated in and around Mannheim, where Karl Benz had first established his gas-engine workshops. In 1910, the company had also acquired the Gaggenau bus and truck works at Baden-Baden, originally created late in the 19th century by Theodor Bergmann to produce the delightfully named Orient Express and Liliput, the latter a cheap 'people's car' long before the advent of the Volkswagen. After a change of direction, the works turned to commercials and a range of more conventional cars—dropped in the slump of 1907–8.

Technological advance, 1914-18

During the conflict, the Daimler and Benz factories had become part of Germany's war machine, turning out military vehicles, aero engines and aircraft. The war temporarily curtailed development of the car but it rapidly accelerated that of the aero engine. In 1913, Benz had won first

30

PAGES 28/29 AND ABOVE *1923–24 Mercedes 24/100/140 Sportwagen. The last figure denotes the 6-litre six-cylinder engine's output with the supercharger engaged. The two-bladed Roots blower came into operation through a multi-disc clutch only when the throttle was fully depressed for brief bursts of extra power.*

RIGHT AND FAR RIGHT *The remarkable 'teardrop' Benz attracted more attention for its unusual design than for its performance on its first appearance at Monza in 1923. With its six-cylinder twin-cam 2-litre engine mid-mounted behind the driver, swing-axle rear suspension, inboard drum brakes and streamlined body, it foreshadowed the shape of things to come. Little more was seen of it on the race tracks, but it did well in hillclimbs with its excellent traction and light weight.*

prize, and Daimler the second-place award, in a competition launched by the Kaiser for an aircraft engine of between 15 and 115 bhp with a power/weight ratio, including sufficient fuel for seven hours, not exceeding 6 kg (13 lb) per horsepower. Competition was intense, with 44 new engines and many developments of existing ones, from 26 German entrants. There were two-strokes, four-strokes, sleeve valves and rotaries with both air and water cooling. Benz's winning entry was a fairly conventional but superbly engineered four-cylinder engine with individual in-line cylinder barrels surrounded by sheet-steel water jackets. A side-mounted camshaft operated overhead valves through pushrods and rockers and the carburettor was enclosed in the crankcase to protect it from temperature extremes. Two high-tension Bosch magnetos fired the cylinders' twin sparking plugs. It was a 100 hp engine of this sort that powered Hellmuth Hirth's monoplane from Berlin to Mannheim—a very long flight for 1913. Later, Benz produced a six-cylinder version.

Daimler, whose second-place engine was also a six, had been powering flying machines since 1899. The weight-saving steel cylinders surrounded by welded-on water jackets—a design first used by Maybach in 1906—and an encapsulated carburettor, became normal aero-engine practice. In 1914, Böhm's 24-hour 12-minute duration flight, and Ölerich's 8100 m (26,575 ft) altitude record were both in Daimler-powered aircraft. To meet the new demands of aerial warfare for faster climbing, higher speeds and greater altitudes by bigger planes, Daimler and Benz both produced normally aspirated and supercharged engines of ever-increasing power: straight sixes, V8s and even V12s developing nearly 600 bhp, though in-line sixes produced by both manufacturers in the 230–250 bhp range were the mainstay of Germany's flying force. In 1915, Daimler also started the manufacture of aircraft at the new Sindelfingen plant, but the end of the war brought this new field of production and technology to a sudden end, and the Sindelfingen factory was turned over to making car bodies.

The first postwar cars
The far-reaching political, economic and social changes caused by the war, succeeded by the total collapse of Germany's monetary system, meant a new approach for the old car manufacturers, if not new models. To begin with, both Daimler and Benz resumed small-scale manufacture of tried and trusted pre-war cars, though evolutionary new models were introduced in the early 1920s. The Benz 10/30 was a modest town and country tourer, also built as a sports car, the 11/40 a six-cylinder variant; the 16/50 was a more luxurious machine that was long-distance tourer or town carriage according to its bodywork. The typical Benz of the early 1920s had a pressed-steel chassis frame with semi-elliptic front and rear springs carrying live axles and wire-spoked steel wheels. There was nothing very special about the engines apart from the fact that they were well engineered and very durable. A chain-driven camshaft operating side valves, magneto ignition, Zenith carburation and force-fed lubrication were typical features. Power was transmitted through a leather-lined cone clutch and a four-speed-and-reverse gearbox to the rear wheels by shaft and bevel gears. Mechanically operated brakes were fitted to all four wheels and the steering was by worm and nut. Electric self-starting, developed in America where there were far more owner-drivers than in Europe, was also now common, and electric lighting, which before the war had been an optional extra, was now standard equipment.

Daimler resumed production with the 28/95, introduced just before the war, and a smaller 16/45 sleeve-valve car, both austerely equipped as certain raw materials, particularly non-ferrous metals, were in short supply. Customers even had to find their own tyres, usually on the black market. It was not until the late 1920s that the technological advances made during the war were reflected in the cars of Daimler and Benz.

with independent swinging rear axles and inboard drum brakes foreshadowed the shape of things to come, though it attracted more attention for its design than its performance on its one works appearance at Monza.

In 1906 Paul Daimler had been succeeded as technical director of the Austro-Daimler works by a brilliant engineer called Ferdinand Porsche. In 1923, when the war-weary Daimler retired as chief engineer at Untertürkheim, it was again the great Ferdinand Porsche who took over from him to head the company's design team. One of his first tasks was to complete the 2-litre straight-eight supercharged racing car, started by Paul Daimler, to replace the 1.5- and 2-litre four-cylinder blown cars that scored a number of successes in the early 1920s. Gottlieb Daimler himself had unsuccessfully tried to force-feed the charge into the cylinder of one of his early engines to improve volumetric efficiency, and L.S. Chadwick in America had built and run a supercharged car in 1907. But supercharging really came into its own during World War 1 as a means of improving power/weight ratios on aircraft and of overcoming the problem of retaining power in thin air at high altitude. Daimler turned to supercharging in 1915; the company probably knew as much about it as anyone when it started blowing some of its car engines after the war.

At the Berlin motor show of 1921, two supercharged models were exhibited: a 10/40/65 with poppet valves, and a sleeve-valve 6/25/40. (The third figure indicates the maximum developed horsepower with the supercharger engaged.) The Roots air pump—two closely meshing figure-of-eight vanes—was mounted vertically at the front of the engine and driven at about three times engine speed from the crankshaft through bevel gears and a small multi-disc clutch which, by means of a mechanical linkage, engaged only when the accelerator was fully depressed. So the supercharger did not operate all the time, but only when extra power was required. In 1922, the now outdated 1914 28/95 was also supercharged for racing, followed by the small 1.5- and 2-litre overhead-camshaft four-cylinder supercharged racers complying with international formulae of the time. Although they were very fast, the 2-litre cars proved difficult to drive and were soundly beaten in the 1923 Indianapolis 500 where Daimler, engaged in an American sales campaign, had hoped to excel. The following year Christian Werner, driving an improved 2-litre four, scored

The return to racing
The war had curtailed all motor racing in Europe but in America, which was not drawn into the conflict until later, Mercedes cars continued to win important races, notably in the hands of Ralph DePalma, who had acquired one of the successful 1914 GP cars. His most famous victory was in the Indianapolis 500 of 1915. After the war, Mercedes soon made their mark again in Europe. Max Sailer, hero of the 1914 French GP, drove a short-chassis 28/95 from Stuttgart to Sicily in 1921 and there won the Coppa Florio, the Targa Florio's companion event for touring cars. The following year Count Giulio Masetti, driving a 1914 GP Mercedes, won the Targa itself against a strong field, including the first of Mercedes' 1.5-litre supercharged racing cars. These little gems contrasted vividly with Count Louis Zborowski's Mercedes-based aero-engined monsters that raced at Brooklands in the 1920s. The first and now legendary 'Chitty Bang Bang' had a Benz engine in a Mercedes chassis. Other cars followed: Chitty 2 was a monster tourer of similar conception; Chitty 3 was based on a 28/95 chassis; and Chitty 4, which had an American Liberty engine in a Mercedes chassis, was later to become 'Babs', the ill-fated car in which the great Welsh engineer/driver Parry Thomas, worthy of better machinery, was killed at Pendine Sands while attacking the world land speed record in 1927.

The Benz company, too, was quick to re-establish its name in racing. A special 10/30 won the first postwar race at the Avus in 1921, and an advanced 'teardrop' twin-cam, six-cylinder, 2-litre, rear-engined racer

a notable double in Sicily, winning both the Targa and Coppa Florio races outright. The company's official records show a total of 93 wins for these 1.5- and 2-litre supercharged cars in 1924, though most of them were in minor events in the hands of privateers, among them a young apprentice called Rudolf Caracciola who was destined for greater things.

Porsche's eight-cylinder 2-litre cars made an inauspicious debut, the whole Mercedes team being withdrawn from lowly positions in the 1924 Italian GP after the popular Zborowski was killed in a crash. Their failure here serves to underline that the Germans were not always invincible first time out. Despite their many victories, neither Mercedes nor Benz really ruled the tracks in the early 1920s. Even if they had not been barred from the French and Belgian classics after the war, it is doubtful whether the four-cylinder Targa cars would have matched the Bugattis, Alfa Romeos and Delages that dominated the 2-litre GP formula. The eight-cylinder cars may well have done so, but by the time they were raceworthy, the new 1926 1.5-litre formula had made them obsolete. Following a lengthy development programme after the Monza debacle, the record of the straight-eight looks good on paper, with 21 wins from 27 starts according to official records. But works drivers Caracciola, Werner and Otto Merz ran in the main against weak opposition. Caracciola's most notable victory was in the first German Grand Prix of 1926 on a wet Avus track where, after a delayed start, he overtook everyone else in the race.

The straight-eight was a potent piece of engineering. Its very stiff built-up crankshaft, running in nine roller bearings, was lubricated by a dry-

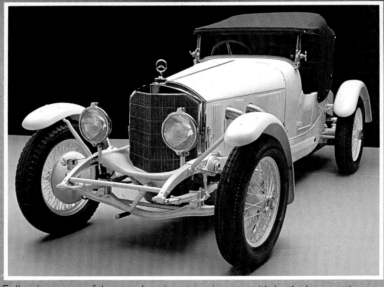

Following successful supercharging experiments with both sleeve-valve and poppet-valve engines, two 'blown' cars were exhibited at the 1921 Berlin show. This superb 1924 10/40/65 sports tourer had a conventional supercharged engine.

sump system and stressed to 6000 rpm. With twin overhead camshafts operating four valves per cylinder, it developed over 160 bhp: rather too much, according to contemporary reports, for the leaf-sprung, live-axled chassis and cable-operated drum brakes. By all accounts, it was a demanding car to drive on the limit, though Caracciola mastered it. Another young German with a flair for organization and attention to detail, who had put in some competent rather than brilliant drives for Mercedes earlier, was at this time appointed to head the racing department. For the next 30 years under the legendary *Rennleiter*, Alfred Neubauer, the Germans really did become all but invincible.

Mercedes built no cars for the 1.5-litre formula, which was dominated by Bugatti as, one by one, other manufacturers withdrew from GP racing because of the prohibitive costs. Sponsorship was a long way off. Dwindling fields forced race organizers to run under Formule Libre rules, and for that Mercedes was ready with its monster supercharged sports cars, developed from the 4-litre 15/70/100 and 6-litre 24/100/140 introduced in 1923. Both were powered by Porsche-inspired straight-six engines, differing only in bore and stroke dimensions, which departed radically from previous design practice. The crankcase and cylinders were a one-piece casting of light alloy; the cylinder barrels and head were of cast iron. A vertical shaft and spur gears drove the overhead camshaft which operated inclined valves by hinged rocker arms and also turned the radiator fan. A light-alloy rocker cover and finned supercharger, integrated with a forward extension of the block/crankcase, force-feeding extra air through the single carburettor, helped to give unusually clean, uncluttered lines. At first, these big, slow-turning supercharged engines powered large, heavy tourers and limousines notable for their comfort and refinement rather than for their speed: a 4-litre Weymann-bodied car tested by *The Motor* in 1924 managed no more than 119.7 km/h (74.4 mph) and took over 20 seconds to reach 60 mph from rest. But they

sired perhaps the greatest series of supercars the world has ever seen, starting with the 24/110/160 K model of 1926 in which Caracciola gave a taste of things to come when he won the Freiburg hill climb in record time.

The merger

The big news of 1926 did not come from the race tracks, though, but from the boardrooms of Daimler and Benz. Amalgamation of the two great rivals had been mooted as early as 1919. By 1923, when both firms were fighting for the same precarious market against crippling economic factors, hostility to the scheme originally proposed by Dr Jahr of Benz had softened. An 'agreement of mutual interest' was signed in 1924 between Daimler Motoren-Gesellschaft and Benz & Cie, and a director of co-ordination appointed. In June 1926, the two companies merged as Daimler-Benz AG.

Although the luxury tax on cars had been reduced from 15 to 7½ per cent, so too had the import duty on foreign cars been cut, allowing fierce home competition. So it was essential to reduce costs and rationalize the range. Production was concentrated on a pair of new Mercedes-designed saloons and tourers: a 2-litre known as the Stuttgart and a 3.1-litre named, inevitably to share the honours, the Mannheim. Coachwork manufacture for the new combine was concentrated at the Stuttgart Sindelfingen works where new presses were installed (the factory is still D-B's main body plant), and the two truck ranges were pruned to avoid duplication. It was also decided to intensify development and production of the diesel engine that Benz had first manufactured in 1909, a decision with far-reaching results, for the Daimler-Benz company was to become world leader in this field.

The encircled three-pointed star of Daimler was combined with the circular laurel wreath (symbolizing victory) of Benz to form a trademark that was soon to stamp its authority throughout the world.

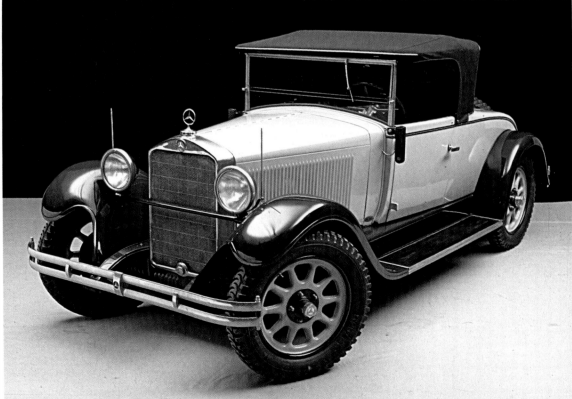

ABOVE *Mercedes made a determined assault on the 1922 Targa Florio with several different cars. Sailer and Werner drove short-chassis 28/95s. Scheef a 1.5 litre supercharged machine, Lautenschlager, Salzer and Count Masetti 1914 Grand Prix models– improved versions of the all-conquering 4.5-litre French GP victors. Masetti, seen here on the tortuous circuit, won the gruelling event.*

LEFT *Following the amalgamation of Daimler and Benz in 1926, the new combine produced two ranges of sound but mundane medium-sized cars powered by six-cylinder side-valve engines. To share the honours the 3.5-litre model was named the Mannheim (where Benz cars were made) and the 2.6-litre the Stuttgart (home of Mercedes). The car shown here is a 1928 Stuttgart 260 tourer.*

Base cars and blowers

For five years after the merger, until 1931, the mainstay of the Daimler-Benz range was the Stuttgart and Mannheim series of medium-sized saloons and tourers. They were dull but dependable cars of conventional design and rather bland styling, recognized by their flat radiators carrying the new emblem, and pressed-steel 10-spoke wheels. They were the last of what the company calls its 'classical' cars, with U-section frames, live axles front and rear supported on leaf springs, and mechanically operated brakes that contemporary road tests criticized as inadequate. The vibration-damped crankshaft of the six-cylinder, wet-liner, side-valve engines—the 2-litre 8/38 and 3.1-litre 12/55—were carried in seven main bearings, so it is not surprising that these heavy, rugged cars were noted more for their smoothness, flexibility and longevity than for their performance. A 2-litre Stuttgart tested by *The Motor* was all out at 75.6 km/h (47 mph), but its very low gearing enabled it to do virtually everything in the highest of its three speeds. The gearbox, operated by a ball-and-socket floor change, drove the 'banjo' live back axle through a propeller shaft enclosed in a torque tube.

More powerful engines were fitted during the course of development to improve the sluggish performance of these respected plodders. The Stuttgart was enlarged to 2.6 litres and became a 10/50, and the Mannheim to 3.5 litres, 14/70. The larger six was later increased to 3.7 litres and supplemented by a sports model called the 370S. In 1928, the 4.4-litre Nürburg 18/80, with an in-line eight-cylinder engine similar in design to the sixes, with the cylinder block and crankcase as one integral casting, was added to the range. When the power was increased to 110 bhp in 1931, this big, refined six-seater became known as the Nürburg 500, but it was never considered a serious rival to, say, the Packard straight-eight outside Germany.

The triumphant supercharged sports cars

These rather dated, live-axled saloons and tourers were Daimler-Benz's bread and butter until the revolutionary 170 series was introduced in 1931. It was the great supercharged sports cars at the other end of the price scale that provided the German jam. A short-chassis version of the big, blown tourer was brought out in 1926. Known as the K (kurz: 'short') model, its 6.25-litre overhead valve six-cylinder engine developed

160 bhp at a lazy 2600 rpm with the supercharger engaged. Its top speed was about 160 km/h (100 mph) but it was the relaxed, long-legged cruising and surging acceleration in top from walking pace that marked it out as something extraordinary. Like other Mercedes cars of the period, though, it had poor brakes—so poor that it became known as the 'death trap'. Even so, it was in a Type K that Caracciola and others started to make an impact in racing and hill-climbing that the heavier, less powerful 24/100/140 had failed to do: a works team of these cars had been humbled by lesser machinery in the touring-car race accompanying the 1926 Spanish Grand Prix.

In 1927, the K was succeeded by the redoubtable 36/120/180, more simply known as the S (for Sport). The enlarged 6.8-litre engine developed 180 bhp and was carried in a chassis that was acutely arched over the rear axle to give a very low centre of gravity and much better handling and roadholding, according to contemporary tests. The car could accelerate swiftly and cleanly from 8 to 170 km/h (5 to 105 mph) in top gear. Still the brakes were the Achilles heel, but that did not prevent Caracciola from winning the opening event on the Nürburgring—beating Christian Werner in one of the eight-cylinder 2-litre grand prix cars in the process. The big names of the Mercedes-Benz team—Caracciola, Werner, Rosenberger, Kimpel and Willy Walb, formerly Benz's ace—scored numerous track and hill-climb victories, not all of them in the big sports cars. Astonishingly, the 1914 French GP-winning car, now with a supercharger fitted by Dr Porsche, was pressed into service and was a formidable contender on the hills. So, too, was the eight-cylinder 2-litre GP car, and a hybrid version of it powered by a 4.5-litre blown 1914 GP engine. The remarkable young lady driver, Ernes Merck, rated by some even more highly than the great Elizabeth Junek, might well have made the Mercedes works team had she not died tragically in 1926 when only 29 years old.

Mercedes was in a strong position by 1928 to capitalize on the poor state of grand prix racing, dwindling fields prompting a switch to Formule Libre rules that allowed in the powerful, supercharged sports cars, now fast enough to take on all comers—and getting faster. The SS, for Super Sports, had a 7.1-litre 225 bhp engine, and the SSK (Short Super Sports) was an even quicker derivative. Caracciola won the 1928 German Grand

Prix on the Nürburgring, where he was the acknowledged master, first time out in the SS, and a few days later gave the SSK a debut victory on the Gabelbach hill climb in record time. Many more wins were to follow.

Although Ferdinand Porsche resigned as joint chief engineer in 1928 to pursue other things, leaving Benz's Hans Nibel in sole charge of design, his supercharged sports cars continued to spearhead an effective German racing programme, reaching their peak in 1930. To underline the competitiveness of the SSK, Caracciola actually led the Monaco Grand Prix on a round-the-houses course for which the big, underbraked sports

PAGES 36/37 *The magnificent 1934 500K Special Roadster, successor to the 380, which had a supercharged straight-eight engine of 5 litres developing 160 bhp.*

LEFT *The supercharged S, introduced in 1927, had a 6.8-litre six-cylinder engine developing 180 bhp. Arching the frame over the rear wheels and using underslung springs lowered the centre of gravity. The car could accelerate from 8 to 166 km/h (5 to 103 mph) in top gear.*

TOP *In 1926 this short-chassis K (kurz, short) was developed from the earlier 24/100/140 supercharged tourer. With an even more powerful 6.25-litre straight-six engine developing 160 bhp at 2800 rpm, it was considered to be one of the most desirable supercars of its day. Even faster blown sports cars were to follow.*

ABOVE AND RIGHT *This 1928 SS, built for singer Al Jolson, was fitted with special sleek bodywork. The SS (for Super Sports) had a 7.1-litre engine developing 200 bhp. It was in a similar car that Caracciola won the 1928 German Grand Prix – the competition debut of the redoubtable SS, which ranks as one of the all-time sports-car greats.*

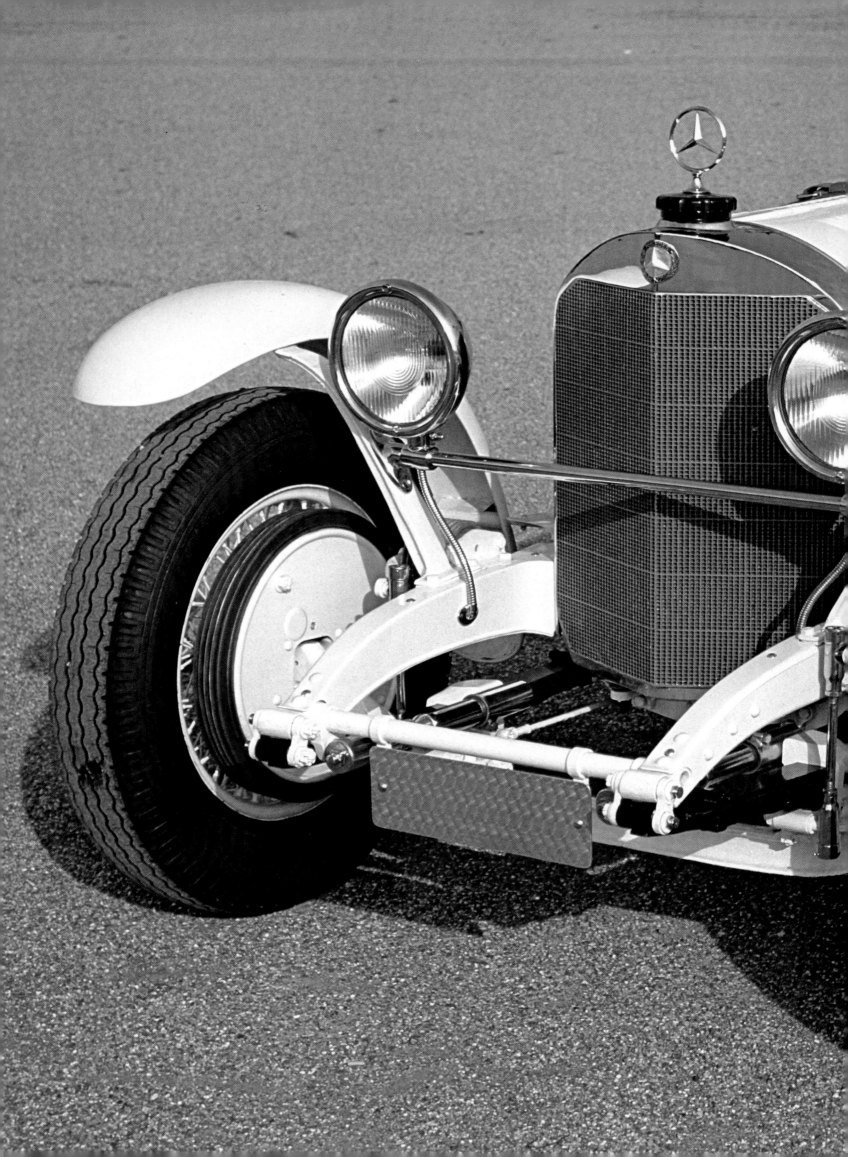

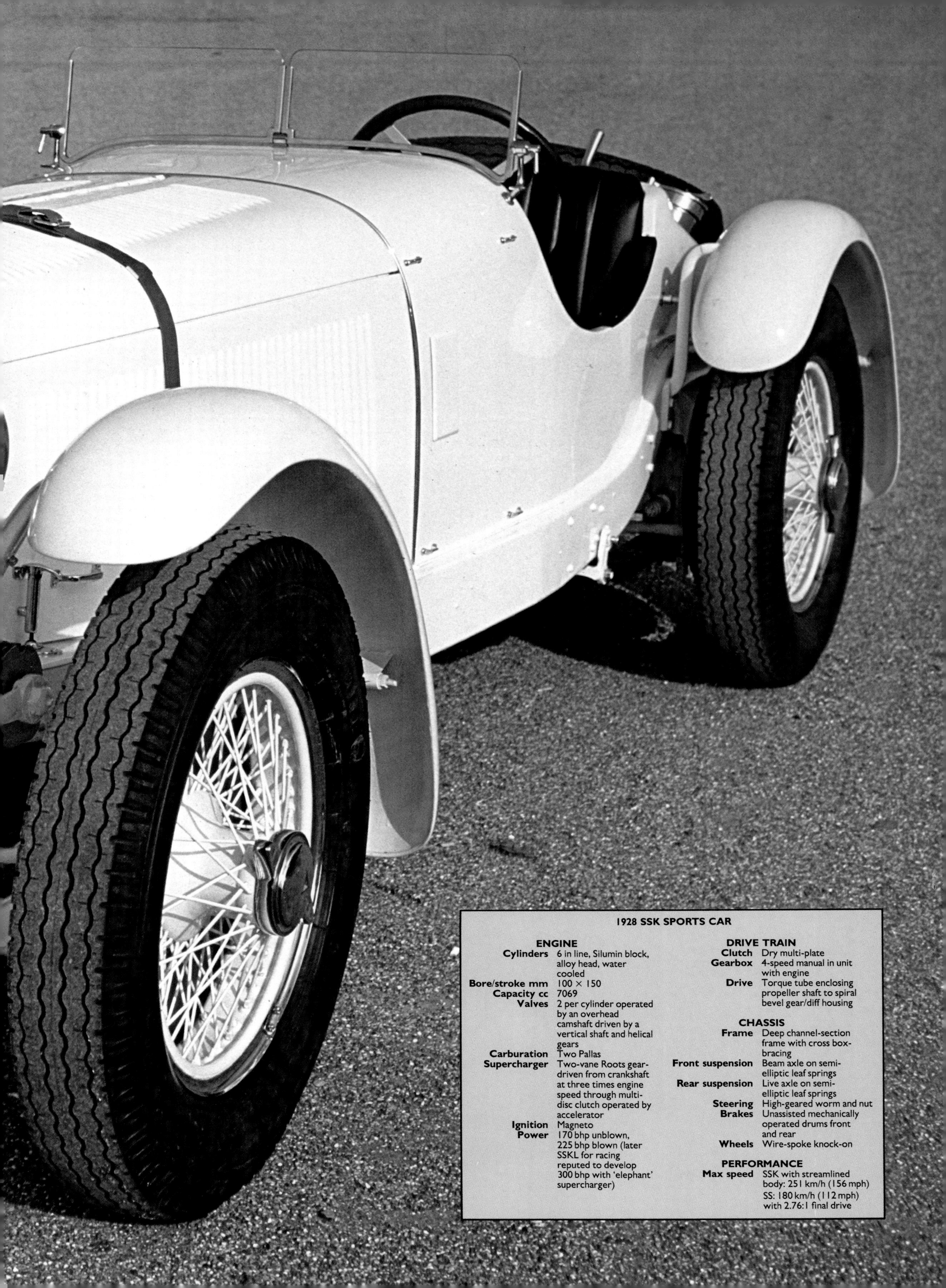

1928 SSK SPORTS CAR

ENGINE

Cylinders	6 in line, Silumin block, alloy head, water cooled
Bore/stroke mm	100×150
Capacity cc	7069
Valves	2 per cylinder operated by an overhead camshaft driven by a vertical shaft and helical gears
Carburation	Two Pallas
Supercharger	Two-vane Roots gear-driven from crankshaft at three times engine speed through multi-disc clutch operated by accelerator
Ignition	Magneto
Power	170 bhp unblown, 225 bhp blown (later SSKL for racing reputed to develop 300 bhp with 'elephant' supercharger)

DRIVE TRAIN

Clutch	Dry multi-plate
Gearbox	4-speed manual in unit with engine
Drive	Torque tube enclosing propeller shaft to spiral bevel gear/diff housing

CHASSIS

Frame	Deep channel-section frame with cross box-bracing
Front suspension	Beam axle on semi-elliptic leaf springs
Rear suspension	Live axle on semi-elliptic leaf springs
Steering	High-geared worm and nut
Brakes	Unassisted mechanically operated drums front and rear
Wheels	Wire-spoke knock-on

PERFORMANCE

Max speed	SSK with streamlined body: 251 km/h (156 mph) SS: 180 km/h (112 mph) with 2.76:1 final drive

PAGES 40/41 *The 1928 SSK (short-wheelbase Super Sports) was an even more powerful version of the SS, with a 225 bhp 7.1-litre blown engine. Caracciola raced such a car with great success despite poor braking.*

ABOVE *Although overshadowed by the big supercharged sports cars, the 3.7-litre six-cylinder Mannheim 370S was admired for its superb looks. The long-bonnet, short-tail styling epitomized design of the 1930s.*

RIGHT *Despite its mundane appearance, the 170 (for 1.7 litres) introduced in 1931 was a radical departure from previous models with its pressed box-section chassis and all-independent suspension.*

car could hardly be less suited. Had it not been for stops for fuel and fresh tyres, which dropped him to third place behind two Bugattis, he might well have won. Later that year, Caracciola scored his famous wet-weather victory in the Tourist Trophy near Belfast against a heavy handicap and a powerful team of blower Bentleys. He had another memorable scrap with Tim Birkin and the Bentley Boys in the 1930 Le Mans 24 hours, but the lone SS shared with Werner eventually retired with electrical trouble. Caracciola's drive in the 1931 Mille Miglia, like that of Stirling Moss for the same team later on, ranks as one of motor racing's epics: in a solo effort dogged by minor problems and against strong opposition, he completed the 1609 km (1000-mile) road race nearly nine minutes quicker than anyone else at an average speed of 101.1 km/h (62.82 mph). Later that year he also won the German Grand Prix at the Avus, once again excelling in the wet.

Although the big blowers were to win many more sports-car and Formule Libre events, they were no match for some of the new thoroughbred single-seaters of the early 1930s like the P3 Alfa Romeo and Type 51 Bugatti. Their last great international victory was in the 1932 Avus race before an estimated 250,000 spectators, when Manfred von Brauchitsch in an SSKL carrying streamlined bodywork designed by an aircraft engineer beat Caracciola—not in his usual Mercedes but at the wheel of an Alfa Romeo—by a mere four seconds. Caracciola was himself

to have driven an SSKL streamliner in the 1933 Eifel race on the Nürburgring but, because of an injury sustained in one of his rare accidents, his place was taken by Otto Merz. In the rain that brought out the best in Caracciola, Merz crashed and was killed. Tim Birkin, co-star of many a Bentley v. Mercedes confrontation with Caracciola, was also to die that year from blood poisoning that developed after burns received in the Tripoli Grand Prix.

The 170 series
In racing, Mercedes was temporarily on the wane, but the company's road-car programme went from strength to strength, and advanced dramatically in 1931 with the introduction of a revolutionary new range of cars designed by Hans Nibel. Both Daimler and Benz had hitherto excelled in engine design but Nibel was first and foremost a chassis man, and it was the all-independently sprung lightweight chassis, first seen at the Paris Salon, that made the new 170, backbone of Mercedes' range for years to come, rather special in its ride and handling.

The Depression had knocked the bottom out of the luxury-car market and the 170 was conceived and built as an advanced contender in the medium-sized, medium-priced sector, a market strongly contested by Mercedes ever since. Its pressed-steel box-section chassis frame was deeply arched over the back wheels to allow ample movement for the

43

ABOVE *Every inch a thoroughbred, its sleek, flowing lines symbolizing power and performance. A 1934 500K Special Roadster with all-independent suspension and a six-cylinder 5-litre supercharged engine.*

LEFT *The short-lived rear-engined 130 saloon. Daimler-Benz's 'people's car', which foreshadowed the Volkswagen, was announced in 1933.*

BELOW LEFT *The 1934 150 sports car had much in common with the rear-engined saloons except that its 55 bhp overhead-camshaft engine was mounted amidships, ahead of the rear wheels.*

RIGHT *Kaiser Wilhelm II's Super (or Grosser) Mercedes of 1932. This enormous live-axled luxury limousine was powered by a supercharged straight-eight engine of 7.7 litres developing 200 bhp.*

PAGES 46/47 *The 500K was superseded by the 540K, with 5.4-litre engine, shown overleaf in four-seater convertible form.* INSET *Massive pontoon wings, each carrying a recessed spare wheel, emphasize the long, sleek bonnet beneath which lies a 160 bhp supercharged engine.*

44

combining inboard coils compressed by upper pivot arms, and a lower transverse leaf spring. Much further up market came the all-independent straight-eight 380 sports tourer with coil-and-wishbone suspension like that pioneered by Cadillac in America. This advanced system, still in use today, separated as three independent elements the wheel location, springing and damping, with consequent benefits to the car's ride and roadholding.

In the late 1920s, Daimler-Benz had constructed some small prototype cars with integral body-chassis units, but financial constraints curtailed development. In 1932, the company also manufactured a small, horizontally opposed four-cylinder engine for a utility runabout. Following these lines of development, which clearly foreshadowed the Volkswagen, the rear-engined 1.3-litre 26 bhp 130 saloon, based on a single-backbone chassis tube, was seen for the first time at the 1934 Berlin show, and was later supplemented by a 1.5-litre, 55 bhp 150 sports car with a mid-mounted engine ahead of the rear wheels. The independent swing-axle rear suspension of these cars was similar to that of the front-engined 170/200 series, and the four-speed gearbox, which was an integral part of the engine, had a semi-automatic overdrive which could be engaged without the clutch.

independent rear suspension. Twin coil springs, one each side of the swinging drive shafts, were anchored under the frame arch. A pair of upper and lower transverse multi-leaf springs located and sprung the independently suspended front wheels. The wishbone arms of the shock absorbers also acted as emergency wheel locators in the event of a spring breakage. The chassis was centrally lubricated and fitted with hydraulic brakes, and an all-synchromesh gearbox, built under Maybach patents, transmitted the modest power of the six-cylinder 1692 cc, 32 bhp side-valve engine to a differential and final drive assembly rubber-mounted to the rigid chassis. Costing £375 in Britain in 1931, the 170 put Mercedes cars within reach of a much wider market. In the next five years, 14,000 170s were made and, from 1932, an even greater number of 40 bhp 200s of similar design. In 1933 came the introduction of the 2.9-litre 290—the policy now was to base model nomenclature on the engine size—in normal and short-chassis form with new independent front suspension

The late 1930s: solid achievement and innovation

Although very advanced, indeed ahead of their time, the small 130/150 cars, supplemented by a 170 version in 1935, did not sell well and were soon dropped from the range. The great success of the 170V, a 1936 development of the original front-engined 170 with a new all-independent X-frame chassis of tubular steel powered by a three-bearing, four-cylinder engine, accelerated the demise of the rear-engined cars. Over 90,000 170V models, the cheapest Mercedes ever built, were sold from 1936 to 1947 with open tourer and saloon bodywork. At the other end of the scale came the mighty Super Mercedes, first produced in 1930 and completely modernized in 1938 with an all-independent chassis, five-speed gearbox and supercharged engine of 230 bhp. The 7.7-litre 770, or Grosser Mercedes, of the late 1930s still ranks as one of the world's great luxury cars.

Capitalizing on its diesel expertise in the light and heavy commercial

ABOVE LEFT *A 1932 170 saloon was dull in appearance but technically quite advanced with its all-independent suspension and six-cylinder engine.*

LEFT *This right-hand drive 1934 500K is still in regular use in England. These great classics are now valuable collectors' cars.*

ABOVE *This 1937 320 four-door saloon has a box-frame chassis carrying all-independent suspension and a 3.2-litre six-cylinder side-valve engine.*

RIGHT *A 1938 230 which, as the nomenclature suggests, was powered by a 2.3-litre engine. It developed 55 bhp and had a top speed of 116 km/h (72 mph).*

fields, Daimler-Benz showed a diesel-engined car at the Berlin show in 1936. Three years earlier, a 3.8-litre, 82 bhp six-cylinder diesel had been fitted to a Mannheim saloon chassis, but the vibration proved too much for it. Further development at the Gaggenau works resulted in the successful 260D, forerunner of Mercedes' highly successful range of diesel cars that were to come later.

From the mid-1930s, Daimler-Benz had the market spectrum well covered, with relatively cheap, everyday models at one end of the range, luxury supercharged limousines at the other, and some worthy middleweights and sports cars in between. The 230, of which 20,000 were made before the outbreak of World War 2, came in 1936 as an up-market version of the 170/200 series, the two- and four-seater models with the new X-frame, and the six-seater saloon with the earlier box-frame chassis like that of the 320. This was a development of the 290 with

3.2 litres and, later on, 3.4 litres (which retained the 320 nomenclature, a confusing anomaly that Mercedes repeated later with several of the postwar models). The big-blower 'vintage' sports cars had given way to the equally coveted all-independently sprung 5-litre, eight-cylinder 500K, with supercharged overhead-valve engine in a luxury sports body, followed later by the even more powerful 2540 kg (2½-ton) 540K with 180 bhp which *The Motor* found gave a top speed of 170.6 km/h (106 mph.) It was one of these monster classics that in 1979 fetched a world record price at auction in America of £200,000.

With the rise of Hitler's Nazi party, Daimler-Benz received the means, through government subsidies, of demonstrating Germany's might and technical prowess on the racing tracks of Europe. It was an invincible onslaught, the like of which the world had never seen—and probably never will again.

The great racers

Caracciola's brief defection to a privately run Alfa Romeo team (in partnership with his friend Louis Chiron) was caused by the temporary shut-down of the Daimler-Benz racing department when it was obvious that the big blown sports cars were no longer competitive against thoroughbred rivals like the 4.9-litre supercharged Bugatti built for free formula racing. The monoposto 2.6-litre Alfa Romeo P3 and the fast-rising Maseratis were also too good for the SSKL, especially on twisty tracks that put heavy demands on brakes and handling. Not that the notoriously underbraked Bugatti was much better than the Mercedes when it came to stopping from high speed. In fact many racing cars of the period had more power than their chassis could safely handle—a familiar story before and since—so the racing authorities introduced a new GP formula for 1934 that, on paper, appeared to resolve the problem without imposing any severe constraints on designers, who were left plenty of scope for ingenuity and inventiveness. It seems doubtful that the Association Internationale des Automobiles Clubs Reconnus (AIACR), the ruling body of the time, appreciated just what could be achieved under a formula that limited the car's weight to a maximum of 750 kg (1653 lb) without water, fuel, oil, tyres or driver, and its body width to a minimum of 85 cm (33½ in).

The W25

With government encouragement and an initial grant of £20,000—a lot of money in those days, though hardly enough to cover what Daimler-Benz had in store—Hans Nibel and his team designed and built the W25 in 10 months. By January 1934 the prototype, which was shown to an approving Hitler, was ready for testing. It is just as well that Nibel was a chassis expert for the key to success was not simply power, for German technology was so advanced and her engine expertise so great that there would be no shortage of that, but how best to use it while keeping the car on the road. Calling on experience gained from the company's all-independent road cars, the W25 had an extensively drilled, lightweight box-section chassis frame with enclosed swinging rear axles pivoted on universal joints each side of the combined four-speed gearbox/final drive assembly. Transverse quarter elliptic leaf springs also helped to locate the wheels. Independent wishbone suspension was used at the front, where bell-crank arms acting on horizontal coil springs enclosed in a chassis cross member helped to minimize frontal area. Friction dampers controlled spring movement at both ends. Unlike most other racing cars of the day, which used mechanically operated brakes, the W25 had a Lockheed hydraulic system to work the big, outboard drums carried by the large wire-spoked wheels. At first, the straight-eight engine had bore and stroke dimensions of 78 × 88 mm to give a capacity of 3360 cc. With a Roots blower running at over twice engine speed, four valves per cylinder operated by twin overhead camshafts, and Bosch ignition, the engine developed 314 bhp in its original form, and 354 bhp when bored to 3.71 litres. In 1935, when the capacity was increased again to 3990 cc, the power went up to a remarkable 430 bhp.

The W25 was a big car, but despite its size it just complied with the 750 kg ruling, thanks to the extensive use of expensive light alloy castings and a no-expense-spared design philosophy. The engine, for instance, was built up from two steel forged blocks welded to cylinder barrels and water jackets to give an immensely strong, rigid but light structure. Even so, it was right on the limit. The story goes that the cars were 1 kg (2.2 lb) overweight at scrutineering for their first serious race. Team manager Alfred Neubauer rose to the occasion. When the cars lined up the following day they were no longer white-painted in the traditional German livery but stripped to bare, glistening aluminium. It was the loss of three pounds of lacquer that gave the cars their respected nickname: Silver Arrows.

Daimler-Benz engineers had considered during the preliminary design stages a rear-engined car. Although attractive in certain respects, it was rejected by Nibel but not by Ferdinand Porsche who now found himself in competition again with his former colleague. Porsche had embarked on an ambitious racing programme instigated by the wealthy privateer, Adolf Rosenberger, who had enjoyed some hill-climbing success in the interesting rear-engined 'teardrop' Benz that first ran at Monza over a decade before. However, the combine of Audi, DKW, Wanderer and Horch, all respected car makers of the day, took over the project as Auto Union, and revealed their Porsche-designed P-wagen at the Avus track in 1934. With nearly 60 per cent of its weight over the back wheels, it had better traction than the Mercedes and although less powerful to begin with—initially its 4.36-litre V16 engine developed 295 bhp—it put more of that power on the road. But the uneven weight distribution, high roll centre created by swinging axles, and far-forward cockpit always made

the Auto Union a tricky car to handle, despite the many improvements that were made to its chassis and suspension over the next five years. Few drivers mastered it, but it was a formidable weapon in the hands of those who did.

Before these two German giants first met—Mercedes under the stern, meticulous, dictatorial Neubauer, Auto Union managed by his old rival Willy Walb—both cars had demonstrated their enormous potential: Caracciola lapped the Avus track at a record 230 km/h (143 mph) and Hans Stuck, whose son also became a grand prix driver, broke three world class records.

In competition, first blood went to Mercedes. In the 1934 Eifel races on the Nürburgring, von Brauchitsch won at record speed after the fiery Italian star of the team, Luigi Fagioli, had retired in a temper following orders to shadow his German team mate. It was not the first time that Fagioli was to clash with Neubauer; but for his great skill, he would probably have lost his place in the team for undisciplined behaviour.

The Germans, still ironing out teething troubles, failed miserably in the 1934 French Grand Prix, which was a walkover for Alfa Romeo, but they were ready again for their own premier event on the Nürburgring in July, though without von Brauchitsch who had broken an arm in an accident during practice. Caracciola led until his car broke down, giving Hans Stuck's Auto Union an easy victory ahead of Fagioli. Caracciola took the Kausen hill climb from Hans Stuck, but the Auto Union driver got his revenge on the Freiburg dash soon after. Stuck was a master on the long Continental hill climbs, which in those days counted towards the European drivers' championship. At Pescara, where Caracciola (who crashed) was timed at 290 km/h (180 mph) it was Fagioli's Mercedes that won; but the Mercedes were outclassed—in fact one of them finished last—in the Swiss Grand Prix at Berne where Auto Union took the first three places.

And so it went on with the now all-conquering German teams sharing the honours, Mercedes taking the Spanish and Italian Grands Prix, Auto Union winning at Brno in Czechoslovakia. In all, the W25 won four of the big internationals in 1934, and rounded off the season with several speed records using a streamlined 3992 cc GP car driven by Caracciola. Significantly, he failed to take the standing-start kilometre from Auto Union, which was quicker off the line thanks to its superior traction, but he

ABOVE *The Italian ace Luigi Fagioli, seen here overtaking Sofetti's Maserati, won the opening round of the 1935 GP season at Monaco. The 430 bhp W25, led by Caracciola, won most of the big events that year.*

PAGES 50/51 *Caracciola hurls the great 1937 W125 through the narrow streets of Pescara.* LEFT *Mercedes' third Monaco win in succession in 1937 was one of the company's most convincing, with W125s finishing first, second and third, led by von Brauchitsch seen here trailing team mate Caracciola who finished second.*

did take the standing mile class record at 188.8 km/h (117.33 mph) as well as the flying kilometre at 317.6 km/h (197.35 mph).

Sadly, Hans Nibel died in November 1934 at the age of 54, so he did not live to see the remarkable 1935 record of the cars he had created. Now with well over 400 bhp and any problems having been sorted out, W25s won nine of the ten big internationals in which they ran, including a one-two-three clean sweep in the French Grand Prix where they had failed so badly the previous year. Caracciola, the star of the team, won five of them. But for a last-lap tyre failure in the German Grand Prix when well in the lead, von Brauchitsch, who had fought off a determined attack from his Mercedes team mates and Auto Union's up-and-coming Bernd Rosemeyer, it would have been ten out of ten. As it was, the legendary Tazio Nuvolari won here by default, albeit after an epic drive, in an Alfa Romeo on one of the very rare occasions during the mid- and late 1930s when a German car did not win a big event. On the basis that as he could not beat them, he might as well join them, Nuvolari was later to race for Auto Union.

The tables were dramatically turned in 1936. By now the Daimler-Benz racing department, with almost unlimited funds (like Auto Union's), employed several hundred people. The W25, with shorter wheelbase, revised suspension, more streamlined body and 450 bhp, was faster than ever and, with two early wins at Monaco and Tunis, appeared set for another invincible season. It was not to be. Thereafter the racing was dominated by the much-improved 16-cylinder Auto Unions, led by the brilliant Rosemeyer; however, a streamlined record breaker, powered by a supercharged 5.6-litre V12 engine, captured several world class records in reaching 366.9 km/h (228 mph) on the Frankfurt–Darmstadt autobahn.

1939 W163 GP CAR

ENGINE

Cylinders	12 arranged in four sets of three forged steel barrels in 60-degree V formation, water cooled
Bore/stroke mm	67 × 70
Capacity cc	2962
Valves	4 per cylinder operated by two overhead camshafts per bank
Carburation	One Mercedes triple-choke
Supercharger	Two Roots in series giving two-stage boost of 2.86 atm (26.5 lb)
Ignition	Two Bosch magnetos, 12 plugs
Power	483 bhp at 7800 rpm

DRIVE TRAIN

Clutch	Single dry plate
Gearbox	5-speed in unit with final drive

Drive	Open propeller shaft to combined all-indirect gearbox/diff and exposed halfshafts

CHASSIS

Frame	Oval tube side members
Front suspension	Independent by coil springs and wishbones
Rear suspension	de Dion tube with torsion bar springs
Steering	Worm and nut, 2¼ turns from lock to lock
Brakes	Lockheed hydraulic finned drums front and rear
Wheels	Wire-spoke knock-on Rudge
Weight	895 kg (1973 lb)

PERFORMANCE

Max speed	315 km/h (196 mph) with highest gearing

The W163, a development of the W154, won five of its seven major races before the outbreak of war. Its 3-litre V12 engine ran to 7800 rpm and developed 483 bhp with two-stage supercharging. Although less powerful than its bigger predecessors, the W163 was virtually as fast thanks to a smaller frontal area, better streamlining and an offset driveline that allowed the driver to sit lower.

The W125

Grand prix racing was to have run under a new 3-litre formula for 1937, and it was for this that the W125 Mercedes was originally designed. But in a late and muddled change, the AIACR extended the 750 kg formula for another year and instead of a 3-litre motor for the 1937 season the W125 appeared with a 600 bhp 5.6-litre straight-eight developed from the W25's. With some 200 bhp more than its predecessor, drastic chassis and suspension changes were called for to utilize all the power, not least to minimize wheelspin, said to be possible at 240 km/h (150 mph) in top in the W25. The light but incredibly strong new oval tube chassis, made of chrome molybdenum steel, carried a torsion bar-sprung de Dion rear axle to keep the driving wheels vertical to the road. The tricky camber changes and high roll centre caused by the old swing-axle design were thus eliminated. Conventional coil-and-wishbone suspension, similar to the successful layout of the 540K, was adopted at the front. With bigger, better brakes and improved transmission, including a ZF self-locking diff, the new car not only had superior traction and roadholding, but was also easier to handle.

It had always been Mercedes' policy to include one or two foreign drivers in the team, and for 1937 the veterans Chiron and Fagioli, the Italian suffering from rheumatism, were replaced by two promising young drivers, the Swiss Christian Kautz and the 24-year-old Englishman, Richard Seaman. The team was led by Caracciola, now at his peak at 36, with the ever-improving Hermann Lang and the Prussian aristocrat von Brauchitsch, who had more than his fair share of mechanical troubles and mishaps, also playing leading roles. It was a long and exciting season, with many memorable races, the honours just going to Mercedes with 7 wins and 9 seconds in 13 races, the fastest of them won by Lang in a special W125 streamliner at the Avus where he averaged 262 km/h (162.6 mph). Auto Union, led by the inspired Rosemeyer, won everything else, including the British Grand Prix at Donington in a year that was totally dominated by the big German cars.

Again, Mercedes rounded off the season with another bag of records. In a new streamlined car powered by the 5.57-litre V12 engine, Caracciola streaked to a new world class record of 433 km/h (268.9 mph), with a one-way best of 436.9 km/h (271.5 mph) on the Frankfurt–Darmstadt autobahn. It was during Auto Union's record attempts that the

ABOVE *Caracciola sweeping to another victory in the 1938 W154, built for the 3-litre formula. Its V12 engine developed 450 bhp. Caracciola won the European drivers' championship for the third year running in W154.*

RIGHT *The 1.5-litre V8 W165, built specially for the 1939 Tripoli GP.*

great racing driver Bernd Rosemeyer was killed when the wind caught his rear-engined streamliner and blew it off course. The narrowness of road gave Rosemeyer no chance of recovery.

The W154

For 1938, the grand prix formula was for 3-litre supercharged cars or 4½-litre unblown ones, with a *minimum* weight limit of 850 kg (1874 lb) with tyres, the idea being to slow the cars down by making them less powerful as well as heavier. Partially to offset the lost capacity, Mercedes increased the engine piston area with a 60-degree V12 supercharged 3-litre, with two overhead camshafts per bank operating four valves per cylinder. The crankshaft and con rods ran on roller bearings and no fewer than nine oil pumps lubricated this masterpiece of engineering. With twin superchargers to increase the boost pressure to 12.25 kg (27 lb), more than double that of the W125, the engine developed 450 bhp at 8000 rpm, and drove the big rear wheels through an open propeller shaft and a five-speed gearbox in unit with the ZF limited-slip differential. The chassis of the new W154 was based on that of the 125, with coil-and-wishbone front suspension and the now familiar de Dion arrangement at the back. As the V12 engine was not as tall as the straight-eight, and angled in the chassis as well, the bonnet line of the new aluminium body was much lower than before.

Although not as powerful as the W125, the W154 was almost as quick, thanks to better handling, brakes and streamlining. It made a bad start though. In the 1938 Pau Grand Prix, the first race held under the new formula, the 4.5-litre unblown V12 Delahaye of René Dreyfus, though a slower car, completed the distance non-stop, and neither Lang nor Caracciola could close the gap on the French car after stopping for fuel. The prodigious fuel consumption of the Mercedes necessitated a huge tankage, which none of the drivers liked.

Thereafter, Caracciola, Lang, von Brauchitsch and Seaman—who won

the German Grand Prix, which was said to have displeased Hitler—had things much their own way on the circuits, if not the hill climbs where Hans Stuck was virtually unbeatable. Without Rosemeyer, though, the Auto Unions were not the force they once were until the little Italian maestro Nuvolari got the hang of the rear-engined monsters and beat the Mercedes in the season's last two grands prix, at Monza and Donington. Even so, out of 10 major events, Mercedes won six and Caracciola, for the third year running, took the European drivers' championship.

The 1939 season started with more world class record runs for Caracciola, this time in a streamlined 3-litre grand prix car which beat Maserati's flying kilometre record by nearly 160 km/h (100 mph) with a speed of over 399 km/h (248 mph). It is perhaps just as well in view of Rosemeyer's fatal accident the previous year that Caracciola was never called upon to drive the monster aero-engined Land Speed Record car, designed for over 650 km/h (400 mph), that Mercedes had built and planned to run on the Frankfurt autobahn. World War 2 put an end to that ambitious project.

The W163

The 154 was replaced in 1939 by the W163 with many detail improvements, a wonderfully sleek new body and some 480 bhp with the help of a new two-stage supercharger that sucked rather than blew through the carburettors. It was a year of triumph and tragedy for the Mercedes team, who won most of the big races. Lang was the undoubted star in this final act but Dick Seaman crashed at Spa while leading the Belgian Grand Prix and died the following day.

Mercedes was not fooled by the Italians' ruse of restricting the prestigious Tripoli Grand Prix to 1.5-litre supercharged cars to give their Alfa Romeos (now led by Enzo Ferrari) and Maseratis what they thought would be an unrivalled run. The Germans wheeled out their superb 1.5-litre V8 W165, designed and built in eight months, and Lang and Carracciola utterly defeated the Italians with their mini-Mercs, beautiful scaled-down versions of the 3-litre 163.

For five years, from 1934 to 1939, German GP cars had ruled supreme. It was another 15 years before the Mercedes were to do so again in grand prix racing.

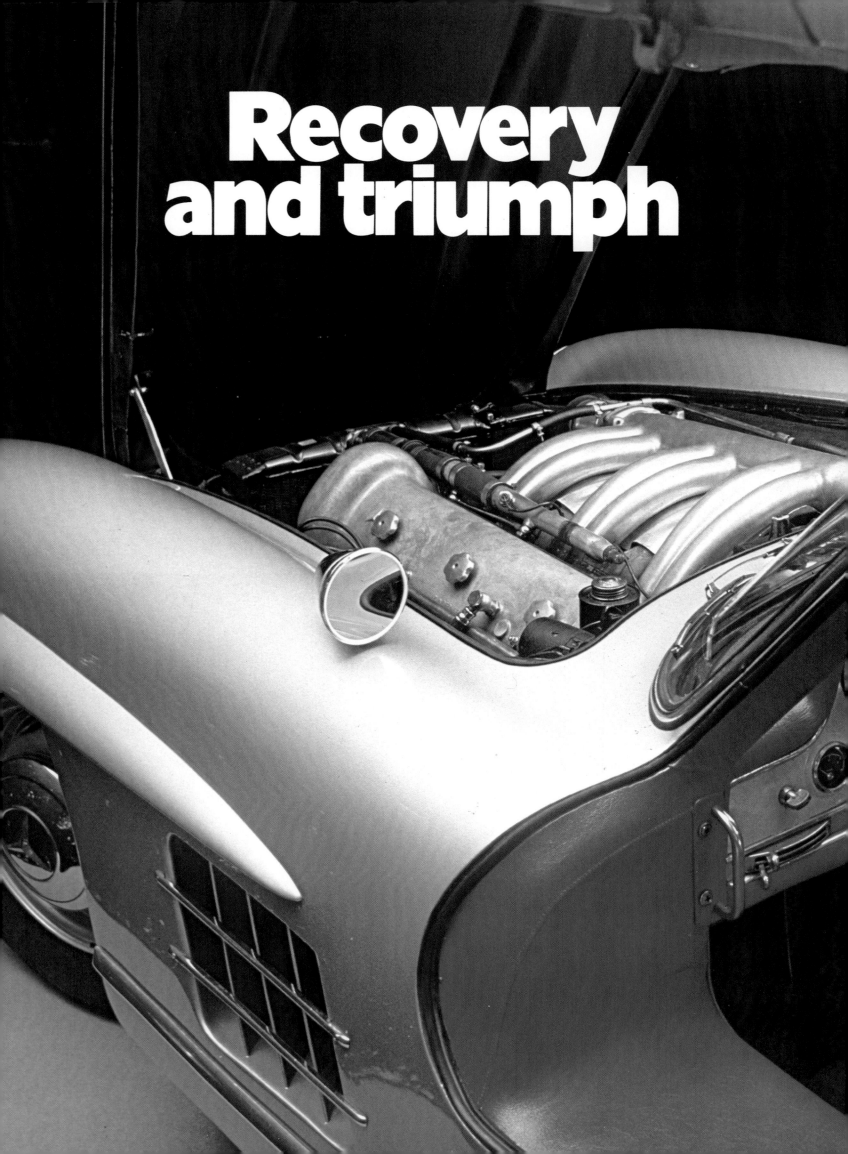

Recovery and triumph

For several years after World War 1, production of aero engines in Germany was restricted to small lightweights like Daimler's popular little 23 bhp horizontally opposed twin. Serious research and development, which did not resume until the amalgamation of 1926, later led to the production of V12s developing up to 1000 bhp for marine and railcar use, as well as for aircraft. Huge 88-litre V16 diesels were also used in naval speedboats and Germany's great airships, including the *Hindenburg* and *Graf Zepplin II*. Later 20-cylinder versions developed 2000 bhp and a supercharged giant over 2500 bhp.

Large-scale manufacture of powerful aero engines started in 1935, following years of development work, when Hitler's Germany was beginning to flex her military muscles. The famous DB 600 series of inverted liquid-cooled V12 engines was the outcome of this work, a specially prepared version of which, developing 2770 bhp at 3100 rpm, powered a Messerschmitt Me 209 V1 to a world record speed of 755.1 km/h (470 mph) in 1939, a figure that was not officially bettered by a piston-powered machine for 30 years, though it is possible that similar speeds were attained by Allied aircraft during and after the war. Many versions of this magnificent engine were made for military use, especially for high-speed fighters, and the development of special fuels, turbocharging, fuel injection and 'double banking' increased power outputs to 3500 bhp.

As in the 1914–18 conflict, development of the car came to a standstill during World War 2 while aero-engine technology advanced dramatically. However, Germany's great expertise in this field was of little immediate help to Daimler-Benz when the crippled company came to pick up the pieces in the spring of 1945. This time, Germany was not only in financial ruin but flattened as well. The factories at Untertürkheim, Sindelfingen and Gaggenau were largely destroyed by Allied air raids, though that at Mannheim escaped the worst of the bombing. For a brief period, Daimler-Benz officially ceased to exist in the immediate postwar period of chaos and disruption, but as the staff filtered back and the lines of communication were re-established, so the round-the-clock job of clearing the debris and rebuilding got under way. It was a monumental task, tackled with typical Teutonic thoroughness and vigour, and it was not long before at least some of the works were operating again, doing general repair and maintenance work.

The 170 series resumed

Car manufacture restarted in 1948 with the pre-war tubular X-frame 170V which, along with the 230 six, had accounted for most of D-B's production in the late 1930s.

In 1949 came the extensively revised 170S that had in fact been running in prototype form, with the works type number of W136, before the war. The modified chassis retained the cruciform layout of oval-section tubes with outriggers to carry the saloon or cabriolet body, but the rear track was increased by nearly 127 mm (5 in) to reduce the tricky effect of swing-axle camber changes, and the old transverse leaf-spring front suspension, which could induce tramp caused by undesirable gyroscopic effects, replaced by a coil-and-wishbone layout similar to that first used on the 540K and GP cars. Improved breathing and a small capacity increase helped to raise power of the 1777 cc side-valve engine by 37 per cent to 52 bhp at 4000 rpm. Even then, the 170S was not a fast car but, thanks to thermostatic control of inlet manifold temperature, a ribbed sump to cool the oil, new lead-bronze bearings for the main and big-end bearings, and fairly high gearing, it could sustain 120 km/h (75 mph) indefinitely on the growing network of autobahns, one of Hitler's few beneficial legacies.

It was the 170S, and the 1700 cc diesel derivative of it, that not only put Mercedes back in big business, but reaffirmed the company's standing as a manufacturer of high-quality cars. *The Motor* was clearly impressed:

> Whether judged from the driving seat or passengers' quarters, this new Mercedes-Benz car offered an almost unique motoring sensation in coupling genuine soft suspension and comfortable ride over rough roads with light precise steering, freedom from roll and an ability to traverse an accurate predetermined course which would do credit to a racing car … Mercedes-Benz have made a very powerful postwar comeback into the motoring world by producing an economical family car of such excellence that new standards of judgement will henceforth be required in this class.

The 220, 300 and 300S

From the 170S, which firmly re-established the three-pointed star as a major automotive force in the late 1940s and early '50s—by 1950 Mercedes was producing 800 cars a week from a workforce of 3200—

the company progressed steadily up-market as the period of hardship and austerity gave way to more affluent times in West Germany's remarkable recovery to prosperity. The 220, introduced in 1951 at the Frankfurt show along with the 300 and 300S, was based on a strengthened 170S cruciform chassis with wider track, powered by a new 2.2-litre six-cylinder engine developing 80 bhp at 4600 rpm. By February 1952, over 1000 a month were being made, prompting *The Autocar* to observe: 'To have repaired the devastation of war and then to have designed, developed and brought to production these three outstanding new models is a great achievement.'

Although it now had faired-in headlights and more room, the first 220 retained the dignified but dated pre-war body styling of the 170. But in its performance and behaviour, it established the character of other Mercedes to follow: its smooth, short-stroke, high-revving engine with a chain-driven overhead camshaft operating staggered valves feeding high-turbulence combustion chambers gave a good specific output at the expense of relatively modest torque at low engine revs. The ability to sustain high cruising speeds without risk of mechanical failure or premature wear stemmed not only from high-quality engineering and manufacture but also from very careful attention to cooling and lubrication. The 220's suspension was similar to that of the 170's, the coil-and-wishbone front end invariably being described in contemporary reports as a direct development of that on the pre-war grand prix cars, adding support to the old adage about racing improving the breed. It would be more accurate, however, to describe the front suspension as an updating of that on the big 540K sports tourer, which was copied on the GP cars.

The bigger 300, again based on the now familiar cruciform chassis and all-independent suspension of coil and wishbones at the front, and swinging half-shafts at the back, represented Mercedes' postwar comeback to the luxury-saloon market, and its more powerful short-chassis derivative, the 300S, carried on the tradition of the great pre-war sports cars. Although they had new conservatively elegant bodywork, their lineage to the pre-war 170 was still clearly evident. Technically,

PAGES 58/59 *Inside the 'gullwing' 300SL. This remarkable closed two-seater coupé, developed from the 1952 sports racing car, was the first production Mercedes to use Bosch fuel injection.*

ABOVE *A 1952 220 drophead. The 220 series had a 2.2-litre high-revving ohc engine which powered a strengthened cruciform chassis carrying dignified but dated bodywork.*

however, they were a major advance on anything that Mercedes had built before, at least in terms of results. The experimental staff demonstrated this by taking one of the big six-seater 115 bhp saloons round the Nürburgring faster than Caracciola had ever done in the supercharged 7-litre SSK. Despite an engine of less than half the size, the 300S was also demonstrably quicker, with a top speed of 175 km/h (109 mph), than the 180 bhp 5.4-litre supercharged 540K of the late 1930s, which weighed well over 907 kg (2000 lb) more than its postwar counterpart.

In the past, Mercedes' production engines had always been very conservatively rated, but the emphasis now on high cruising speeds from relatively small, economical and efficient engines resulted in dramatically improved power/weight ratios and higher specific outputs. The pre-war 170V, for instance, developed 22 bhp/litre, the new 300S 49.5 bhp/litre, indicating a fresh line of thought in keeping with European trends by the engineers now in charge, Fritz Nallinger and Rudolf Uhlenhaut: though in chassis design Mercedes cars of the period still reflected the influence of the far-sighted Hans Nibel who had died in 1934.

Like the 220, both the 300 models had four-speed manual gearboxes operated by a column-mounted lever, an American development fashionable at the time, and numerous ingenious refinements, like the use of a telescopic damper in the steering linkage to minimize kickback, and a driver-controlled servo mechanism to stiffen the rear suspension for heavy loads.

Uhlenhaut was not only a gifted engineer but a driver of some repute. The story goes that before the war he had been soundly admonished by his superiors not just for test-driving the racing cars, but for doing so at

speeds that rivalled the team's aces. As head of research and development, Uhlenhaut was responsible for the postwar racing programme, resumed under Neubauer's direction in 1951 soon after the ban on Germany's participation in international events was lifted. A three-car team of pre-war 3-litre W163s was entered for the Argentine Grand Prix, more to test the organization than the machinery for the cars, now 12 years old, really had nothing to prove. Even so, they finished second and third to Gonzalez' Ferrari. A team of 300s, which included Lang and the veteran Caracciola—Mercedes remained very loyal to its pre-war stars—won the Charles Faroux manufacturers' team award in the 1952 Monte Carlo Rally, indicating that Neubauer's department was once again running smoothly and efficiently and was ready for sterner tests.

The 300SL and the return to racing
It was the six-cylinder engine of the 300S that provided the basis for Mercedes' long-rumoured comeback to European racing in 1952 with the 300SL, or 3-litre Sport Leicht to interpret the nomenclature. And light it was, with a small, closed coupé body with gullwing doors clothing a space-frame chassis of thin steel tubes powered by an inclined (for a low bonnet line) development of the 300S engine with raised compression and three downdraft Solex carburettors, developing a relatively modest 175 bhp at 5200 rpm. The suspension was similar to that of the production cars; even the flexible kingpost mounting, which allowed slight fore and aft cushioning of the front wishbones, was retained, though the car had bigger drum brakes and a close-ratio four-speed gearbox.

Modest or not, the 300SL was strong, well engineered and very successful. If not the fastest sports car of its day, it could certainly claim to be the most dependable and best supported, paving the way for greater things to come. Of the five events in which it was entered in 1952 before being withdrawn, the 300SL won four. Its only 'failure' was on its difficult debut in the Mille Miglia when Karl Kling and Hans Klenk, newcomers to the team, finished an honourable second to Giovanni Bracco's Ferrari, with Caracciola (a past winner) and Kurle fourth. In the Grand Prix de Berne, Kling, Lang and Fritz Riess took the first three places after the only

serious opposition—a works-supported 4.1-litre Ferrari—had failed on the line with a broken transmission. Caracciola was injured in a crash just before the end in what proved to be his last appearance in the Mercedes racing team, so he did not compete in the 1952 Le Mans soon after. While Jaguar, Cunningham, Ferrari, Talbot and Gordini fought for the lead in the 24-hour race, the three Mercedes coupés gave a demonstration run in regularity and reliability, gradually climbing the leader board as faster cars failed until only the 4.5-litre Talbot, driven solo by the Frenchman Pierre Levegh, was ahead. Within sight of victory after an epic drive, his Talbot ran a big end, handing the race to the 300SL of Kling and Klenk.

The Germans were not represented in their own 1952 Grand Prix, a walkover for Ferrari, but in the accompanying sports-car race 300SLs, some with open bodies, filled the first four places. The fifth and final appearance of the little gullwings was in the gruelling Mexican Pan Americana, success in which would mean a boost in prestige and sales in the United States. Again Ferrari fielded the fastest car, Mille Miglia winner Bracco building up a useful lead. But in the end it was the 300SL's reliability, Neubauer's slick organization and the dependable Kling and Klenk that won the day again for Mercedes.

There was certainly an element of luck in the 300SL's 1952 successes. It could so easily have been reduced to a respectable placing at Le Mans had faster cars not failed, and there was little to oppose it at Berne where, as in the Pan Americana, less fragile Ferraris might well have beaten it—as one did in the Mille Miglia. But the Mercedes company had made its point: without the fastest car, it had fielded a winner in what was really little more than a trial run for a bigger onslaught to come.

In 1953 the factory withdrew from racing, but that was not the end of the 300SL. Far from it. Capitalizing on its victories, particularly in America, Mercedes introduced a limited production 300SL that retained several of the competition version's unusual features, including the gullwing doors and removable steering wheel that facilitated entry and exit. Its big advantage over the racers, though, was in the first-time use of Bosch fuel injection, developed from that of the aero engines. With improved induction and optimum fuel-air mixture throughout all operating

conditions, allowing the use of a higher 8.55:1 compression ratio, the power of the seven-bearing, dry-sump overhead-cam 3-litre six was increased to 215 bhp at 6200 rpm, 40 bhp more than the racing cars developed with Solex carburation. With the highest of three possible axle ratios, intermediate maxima were 82, 138 and 203 km/h (51, 86 and 126 mph), with a top speed of over 258 km/h (160 mph): astonishing figures for 1954, though clean aerodynamics and an inclined engine that gave a very low frontal area were in part responsible for the car's great speed. The Bosch injection also made it very docile, with the ability to accelerate cleanly from 24 km/h (15 mph) in top gear on low-grade petrol.

Like the racer, the production two-seater was based on a spaceframe structure of small-diameter tubes with the now traditional Mercedes coil-and-wishbone front suspension and swinging rear axles, which could make the car tricky to handle in unskilled hands. Although disc brakes were being tried and developed elsewhere to good effect, Mercedes stuck to traditional methods, advancing the technology in that field about as far as was possible with radially finned aluminium-cased drums.

The high price (nearly £4400 in Britain in 1954) put this low-volume German supercar beyond the reach of all but the influential rich.

The 190SL and the 180

It was with the relatively humdrum companion 190SL (1.9-litre Sports Leicht) that Mercedes attacked the volume specialist market. Although the hood, windscreen and bumpers could be removed, and the doors replaced with lightweight cutaway ones for competition use, the 190SL was much more of a civilized open tourer than an out-and-out sports car, even though its dry-sump engine—basically an ohc 300 six with two cylinders removed to make a four—developed a respectable 110 bhp at 5500 rpm with two horizontal Solex carburettors, to give a maximum speed of 190 km/h (118 mph). Although the wheelbase was the same as the 300SL's, the track even wider, and the body styling strongly reminiscent of the open 300SL racers of 1952, the 190SL was in fact based on the chassis of the new 180 saloon, introduced in 1953.

The advantages of an integral body-chassis unit, among them great

1954 220	
ENGINE	
Cylinders	6 in line, water cooled
Bore/stroke mm	80 × 72.33
Capacity cc	2195
Compression ratio	6.5:1
Valves	2 per cylinder operated by single overhead cam.
Carburation	Single Stromberg
Power	80 bhp at 4750 rpm
DRIVE TRAIN	
Clutch	Single dry plate
Gearbox	4-speed all-synchromesh in unit with clutch/engine
Drive	Propeller shaft to final drive/diff unit and swinging axles
CHASSIS	
Frame	Separate tubular steel backbone chassis frame
Front suspension	Independent by coil springs and wishbones
Rear suspension	Independent by swing axles and coil springs
Steering	Recirculating ball
Brakes	Hydraulically operated drums front and rear
Wheels	Pressed steel disc
Weight	1360 kg (2998 lb)
PERFORMANCE	
Max speed	129 km/h (80 mph)
Acceleration	0–60 mph 21.8 sec

ABOVE *The styling of this 1954 220 Coupé reflects that of the pre-war 170 convertible. It had a modern six-cylinder ohc engine.*

LEFT *The 300S of the mid 1950s had several advanced features, including single-joint swing axle rear suspension.*

strength from a lightweight structure, were being widely exploited by other manufacturers in the early 1950s, but all postwar production Mercedes cars had hitherto been based on the separate cruciform oval-tube chassis first seen in 1936. The 180 represented a radical departure from that design, with a pressed-steel floorpan stiffened by a central backbone and boxed side members, integrated with a full-width five-seater body of modern design. A subframe carrying the engine, gearbox and front suspension insulated the running gear from the body structure through rubber bushes to reduce the transmission of noise and vibration, an innovation that impressed the testers of *The Motor:* 'This unusual arrangement, plus the quietness of the transmission and the lack of wind noise, combine to make this a notably smooth and quiet car especially in the range of speeds between 30 and 60 mph.' However, the retention of the old-fashioned side-valve engine, still giving 52 bhp, underlined that

although a much roomier, more comfortable and refined car than the 170 series, it was no great performer. Quiet and economical yes, fast no. *The Autocar* got 115 km/h (71.4 mph) and 0–97 km/h (0–60 mph) in 29.9 seconds from their press demonstrator in 1954 when the price with tax in Britain was £1694.

The 180 was soon followed by the 220a using an improved 85 bhp 220

1955 300SL

ENGINE

Cylinders	6 in line, canted block, water cooled
Bore/stroke mm	85 × 88
Capacity cc	2996
Valves	2 per cylinder operated by chain-driven overhead cam.
Compression ratio	8.55:1
Induction	Bosch fuel injection
Power	215 bhp at 6200 rpm

DRIVE TRAIN

Clutch	F and S single dry plate
Gearbox	4-speed all-synchromesh in unit with clutch/engine
Drive	Single propeller shaft to hypoid bevel axle

CHASSIS

Frame	Triangulated tubular spaceframe
Front suspension	Independent by coil springs and wishbones
Rear suspension	Independent by low-pivot swing axles
Steering	Recirculating ball
Brakes	Hydraulically operated finned drums front and rear
Wheels	Steel disc with knock-on hubs
Weight	1020 kg (2249 lb)

PERFORMANCE

Max speed	265 km/h (165 mph) with 3.25:1 final drive
Acceleration	0–60 mph 7.2 sec

The 300SL, shown here in 1955 guise, was arguably the greatest of the exotic sports cars of the 1950s. It was not only sensationally fast but also very docile, its Bosch-injected six-cylinder engine pulling from under 32 km/h (20 mph) in top gear. The sleek two-seater closed body was carried by a lightweight spaceframe with coil and wishbone front suspension and swinging rear axles that made the car tricky to handle on the limit.

six-cylinder overhead camshaft engine with better low and mid-range torque in a roomier integral body-chassis unit based on the 180's. Effectively increasing the length of the drive shafts by doing away with the pivot each side of the final drive assembly and introducing instead a single central joint, reduced camber changes of the rear wheels still further. This design, which gave better roadholding and safer handling (even in the mid-1950s swing-axle suspension had its critics) was soon adopted on the 180.

So, by 1955 Daimler-Benz was firmly re-established as the manufacturer of a wide range of quality cars, including the 170/180 four-cylinder petrol and diesel saloons, the faster up-market 220a six based on the 180 shell, the luxury 300 saloon and 300S tourer—both dignified and desirable though by now rather dated—and the ultra-modern 190SL and 300SL sporters. Besides all the cars, there was also a big range of commercials, from flat-nosed lightweight vans to long-nosed heavy trucks, not to mention the Universales Motorgerät, shortened to Unimog, an all-purpose, go-anywhere, do-anything four-wheel-drive truck-cum-tractor, first seen at the Frankfurt agricultural show in 1948 and subsequently developed into a workhorse of astonishing versatility.

It was to underline the engineering skills of Daimler-Benz and to promote the name of Mercedes throughout the world with an impact that no advertising campaign could have achieved that the company returned to big-time motor racing in 1954, following the successful foray with the 300SL two years before and a research and development programme that had started long before that. Chief engineer Fritz Nallinger observed that lessons learned in racing, the most challenging test of engineering skills, inevitably rubbed off on the road cars. It brought out the best from everyone concerned, and nothing but the best was going to be good enough to achieve the sort of invincibility that Mercedes had demonstrated more than once before.

RIGHT *The elegant, unaggressive styling of the 300SL belied the great performance of this low-volume supercar.*

BELOW *A 1961 190SL. It was with this wide-track model, more open tourer than out-and-out sports car, that Mercedes attacked the specialist market in the 1950s and early '60s. Its engine was basically a four-cylinder version of the 300SL's 'six'.*

Back to the track

PAGES 68/69 *The 1955 300SLR sports racer was based on the W196 grand prix car, not the earlier 300SL gullwing machine. Its straight-eight fuel-injected 3-litre engine, mounted on its side to give a low bonnet line, developed almost 300 bhp.*

ABOVE AND RIGHT *The W196, built for the 1954 2.5-litre GP formula, first appeared with all-enveloping streamlined bodywork (see page 73) but the car scored most of its wins as an open-wheeler like this. The lightweight spaceframe chassis carried all-independent suspension and a straight-eight engine with desmodromic valve gear.*

The Daimler-Benz concern committed itself to an ambitious and astronomically expensive grand prix racing programme in 1952 when the new 2.5-litre formula, effective from 1954, was announced. Lessons learned from the 300SL, even less from the all-conquering pre-war racing cars, were of little value for a new Formula 1 machine that *had* to be capable of winning from the start. Rather than produce a carbon copy of the dominant Italian Ferraris and Maseratis, which would no doubt have worked but offered insufficient scope for development, the Mercedes designers characteristically shunned current GP design practice and started from scratch, basing their ideas on a great deal of original research and calculation.

Despite Mercedes' unparalleled experience with supercharging, the alternative 750 cc blown engine permitted by the new regulations was ruled out at a very early stage. Even to Untertürkheim it looked a non-starter. Impossibly high revolutions, piston speeds and boost pressures from power-guzzling multi-stage compressors would be needed to achieve the minimum 400 bhp/litre considered necessary to make the engine competitive. Even then, reliability of such a highly stressed unit would be a major headache and the engine would be short on torque and high on fuel consumption. What is more, a diminutive multi-cylinder supercharged engine would have little bearing on anything Mercedes built for the road and was therefore considered of little commercial or technical value.

The new straight-eight and the W196

The new unit therefore had to be an unblown 2.5-litre: but of what configuration? Mercedes examined several alternatives, including V8s and V12s like the highly successful pre-war racing engines. After all, the greater the number of cylinders, the better the volumetric efficiency and thus power output. But despite a worldwide trend towards V-type engines, Mercedes rejected this layout because the duplication of auxiliary drives for the valve gear meant unnecessary weight, and opted instead for a straight-eight which, if laid on its side, had the added advantage of being very shallow, allowing a very low bonnet line. The engine was in effect two back-to-back 'fours' with a central gear train to drive the two overhead camshafts, as well as a central power take-off to eliminate torsional vibrations in the long built-up crankshaft running in 10 roller bearings and carrying forged con rods in ball races. A geared-down subshaft from this central delivery transferred the drive to the clutch and rear-mounted five-speed gearbox.

In its construction the engine followed traditional Mercedes practice, with one-piece forged cylinder bores and combustion chambers, welded together in groups of four, with the ports welded on top of the hemispheres and then surrounded by welded-on steel-sheet water jackets. The invincible 1914 GP engine had been built along similar lines. In detail design, though, the new straight-eight broke fresh ground. Instead of the expected four small valves per cylinder disposed at 60 degrees, there were only two large ones at an included angle of 90 degrees, positively opened *and* closed by a unique and ingenious desmodromic arrangement of cams and rockers, removing the need for space-consuming return springs and the limitations they impose on valve lift and peak accelerations. By eliminating the risk of a destructive encounter between valves and pistons during, say, a missed gear change, safe engine speeds of up to 9000 rpm were possible, though this was a useful bonus rather than a design objective. The primary purpose of the desmodromic valve gear was optimum filling of the combustion chambers. Writing in *The Motor*, Dr Ing. H. Scherenberg, who did much of the preliminary research on the W196, said: 'With this arrangement it became possible to arrive at such generous valve openings that even better conditions than those obtaining on a 12-cylinder engine with normal valve gear could be achieved.'

One predictable carry-over from the 300SL was the use of Bosch direct fuel injection, with the nozzles placed some way down the cylinder bores so that they were protectively shrouded from intense thermal loads by the pistons at the moment of ignition.

By laying the engine almost on its side the W196 had a very low build and centre of gravity. Like the 300SL, the lightweight spaceframe was constructed from small-diameter tubes, suspended at the front by upper and lower wishbones fabricated from the solid in Mercedes' traditional way. The rear suspension raised a few eyebrows, though. Instead of the de Dion layout, pioneered on pre-war Mercedes GP cars and by the 1950s almost standard practice for racing machinery, Daimler-Benz reverted to a sophisticated and unusual swing-axle design, which could at least be related to that of the latest road cars. The wheels were laterally located by curved arms swinging from a common, low central pivot beneath the rear gearbox casing only a few inches above the ground, thus effectively increasing the radius of the swinging arms to reduce wheel-camber changes, as well as lowering the car's roll centre. Fore and aft location was by upper and lower longitudinal arms forming a Watts linkage. As at the front, springing was by torsion bars, not because of any innate advantage conferred by this medium but because there was really no room for anything else. The brakes, too, were a surprise. The factory had always mistrusted anything it had not developed itself, so rather than risk disc brakes, still in their infancy but showing great promise elsewhere, the racing department opted instead for tried and trusted drums, albeit very sophisticated ones developed from those of the 300SL, with an inner cast-iron ring bonded to a light-alloy drum, heavily finned to dissipate heat. To minimize unsprung weight, these huge drum brakes were mounted inboard, driven at the front by shafts from the wheels.

Few of these technical details were known when pictures of the car were first released early in 1954: what attracted most attention then was the sleek, incredibly low, all-enveloping streamlined bodywork. Mercedes had recognized early in the development programme that efficient aerodynamics, evolved from wind-tunnel tests, would help them win races on fast circuits: and the first on which they were to compete, at Rheims for the 1954 French Grand Prix in July, was very fast indeed. Even so, Mercedes left nothing to chance for Neubauer had recruited as his number one driver the great Argentinian maestro, Juan Manuel Fangio.

The W196s on the circuits

Although Alberto Ascari's open-wheel Maserati was only a fraction of a second slower than the Mercedes streamliners in practice, Fangio and Kling ran away from the Italians in the race, the Ferraris of Froilan Gonzalez (leading the chase) and Mike Hawthorn both retiring. This memorable debut victory pointed towards the sort of invincible comeback that the pundits had forecast. Yet three weeks later the Mercedes were soundly trounced in the British Grand Prix at Silverstone. Although Fangio started from pole position, it was the Ferrari of Gonzalez that set the pace. In the heat of battle Fangio found the W196 a bit of a handful, and on more than one occasion hit the circuit marker barrels that were hard to see from the central cockpit of the low-slung streamliner. Fangio dropped even further back after a mid-race downpour, eventually to finish fourth, with team mate Kling a lowly seventh. The opposition took heart. The new Mercs were not, after all, unbeatable, though the Silverstone debacle was arguably the result of a tactical error in using enclosed cars on a circuit for which they were unsuited, rather than the squat open wheelers which the drivers preferred. These were raced for the first time in the German GP on the Nürburgring. Fangio, Kling and Lang were entrusted with the new cars, aesthetically less pleasing than the enclosed streamliner that Herrmann drove, but demonstrably more effective on this sort of track. Even so, only Fangio made the front row of the grid, shared with Hawthorn's Ferrari and Moss's Maserati. It was not the dogfight between the Italian and German cars that made this a

memorable race, however, so much as the meteoric drive of local hero Kling who, starting from the back row after missing official practice, swept through the field to overtake Fangio for the lead. After breaking the lap record several times, he unfortunately also broke his car and eventually finished fourth, much to the displeasure of Neubauer who had planned on a clean sweep in front of the home crowd.

Fangio won again in the Swiss Grand Prix, though Moss had beaten him in a wet practice session and was already attracting the attention of Neubauer, just as Dick Seaman had done in the late 1930s. Nor were the works Ferraris by any means outpaced. The Mercedes team was certainly having to work for its wins, never more so than in the Italian Grand Prix at Monza where Ascari's Ferrari led Fangio until Stirling Moss overtook them both to hold the lead for 45 laps until his Maserati failed within sight of victory. Ascari also retired, so once again Fangio took the chequered flag

RIGHT *Hermann Lang in a 1954 W196 streamliner on the Nürburgring, a twisty circuit better suited to the more wieldy open-wheel cars.*

BELOW *Juan Manuel Fangio (2) and Stirling Moss head the field at Monaco, 1955. Both retired.*

for his fourth win of the season. This was Mercedes' last GP victory that year. In the Spanish event at Barcelona, it was the new and very fast F1 Lancias that set the pace until they retired, leaving Fangio to contend not only with other Italian cars ahead but a tiresome wind that whisked leaves and waste paper into the radiator air scoop, causing the engine to overheat and spew oil. He eventually finished fourth behind Hawthorn's winning Ferrari.

In its first season, the W196 had proved itself to be fast and reliable— but not unbeatable. Had it not been for the driving talents of Fangio, the record books might well have shown a very different story. Nevertheless, a Mercedes had helped to carry Fangio to his second world title, and Daimler-Benz, largely through the Argentinian's efforts, clinched the manufacturers' championship. After such a long lay-off from grand prix racing, it was a pretty devastating comeback.

The 300SLR
With a season's valuable experience behind the team, lighter and more powerful cars, and Stirling Moss now enlisted to support Fangio, it was hard to see who or what could beat Mercedes in 1955. In addition, Daimler-Benz now had a second Silver Arrow to a powerful bow in the shape of the 300SLR (designated the W196-S), a derivative of the grand prix machine rather than a development of the gullwing 300SL racer of 1952, to contest the great sports-car classics. Like the W196, the 300SLR had a straight-eight inclined engine with desmodromic valve gear and fuel injection. But instead of forged fabricated cylinder barrels, the cylinder block was cast in light alloy with chrome-plated bores. Bore and stroke dimensions were greater than those of the 2496 cc GP engine, giving a capacity of 2976 cc. Valve timing, too, was altered to provide greater mid-range torque (220 lb ft at 5950 rpm) at the expense of absolute power (296 bhp at 7450 rpm). In chassis, suspension and brake design, the 300SLR was very similar to the grand prix car, though the spaceframe chassis (weighing a mere 59.8 kg—132 lb!) was a little wider to accommodate two people, and the inboard front brakes, driven by angled double-jointed shafts, were moved slightly forward so that the engine could be mounted further forward too. Outboard front brakes (to allow a shorter wheelbase on twisty circuits) were also available. So, too, was a novel hydraulically operated air brake that flipped up behind the driver's
74

head for especially demanding braking from high speeds, like that needed at the end of the Mulsanne straight at Le Mans where the 300SLR could reach 290 km/h (180 mph).

Mercedes started the year in fine style in South America, Fangio winning the Argentine Grand Prix in January, and the Buenos Aires GP (a non-championship race) two weeks later from Moss. The European campaign began in May with the famous victory of Stirling Moss in the Mille Miglia, navigated by journalist Denis Jenkinson from a roller map of pace notes. Moss's average speed of 157.2 km/h (98 mph) in the debut appearance of the 300SLR was 16 km/h (10 mph) faster than the race had ever been won before, and not even Fangio—driving solo even though he did not much care for sports-car racing—could match the pace of the young British ace. He finished 30 minutes adrift in second place after the fast but fragile Ferraris of Piero Taruffi and Eugenio Castellotti had given up. It was an epic win for Moss.

For a time it looked like yet another Mercedes one-two walkover in the Monaco GP three weeks later for Fangio and Moss, both driving W196 open wheelers with outboard front brakes in order to shorten the chassis for the twisty Monte Carlo circuit. The two German cars were well ahead of the Lancias and Ferraris but to the astonishment of everyone, not least Neubauer and his pit crew, both cars suddenly failed: Fangio's with transmission trouble, Moss's with a blown engine. Not even Mercedes cars were infallible. A week later the team's spirits were back to their normal level when Fangio and Moss almost dead-heated their 300SLRs in the Eifelrennen on the Nürburgring, and early in June they scored another one-two in the Belgian Grand Prix.

The Le Mans tragedy and its aftermath
Things were now running pretty well according to plan again for Mercedes until that fateful moment on 11 June 1955 when poor Pierre Levegh, invited to join the 300SLR team at Le Mans as a tribute to his epic drive two years before when he so nearly beat the 300SL, cannoned off a slower car in front of the pits and scythed into the packed terraces. Over 80 people, including Levegh, died in the worst accident in motor-racing history. At 2 am, orders were received from Stuttgart to withdraw the remaining cars as a mark of respect when Moss and Fangio had a two-lap lead over the disc-braked D-type Jaguar of Hawthorn and Ivor Bueb with

ABOVE *The lightweight spaceframe chassis of the 1955 300SLR was clothed with a low-slung aluminium body. On its memorable debut, Stirling Moss won the Mille Miglia at record speed with journalist Denis Jenkinson navigating from a roller map. Although both are small men, there was little room to spare in the cramped cockpit.*

RIGHT *The air-braked 300SLR of Fangio battled it out nose-to-tail with Hawthorn's Jaguar D-type (6) for the first two hours of the 1955 Le Mans 24 marathon. Later, when the Fangio/Moss car was well in the lead, the Mercedes team was withdrawn after team mate Levegh had cannoned into the packed terraces, killing over 80 people.*

which Fangio had had a titanic battle in the opening two hours.

The Le Mans tragedy, through no fault of Mercedes, cast a shadow over motor racing for a long time afterwards. Switzerland was never to hold another motor race and the 1955 French and German Grands Prix were cancelled, though such was the form of the W196 and its two ace drivers that it is hard to imagine anything but a Mercedes winning either. To underline the point, the German cars finished first and second in the next three GPs to be held—Fangio, Moss at Zandvoort in the Dutch GP; Moss, Fangio in a photo finish at Aintree in the British GP; and Fangio, Taruffi in Italy's premier event at Monza where Fangio and Moss (who retired) once again drove enclosed streamliners.

The end of works-supported racing

Nothing could stop the 300SLR either. In the Swedish GP at Karlskoga, Fangio and Moss took the first two places in another photo finish driving air-braked cars; and Mercedes were first, second and third in the Dundrod Tourist Trophy after the Jaguar and Aston Martin challengers had wilted. In a bid to wrest the sports-car championship from Ferrari— the F1 drivers' and constructors' titles were already in the bag—Neubauer dispatched two 300SLRs to Sicily for the Targa Florio. When Moss went off the road and lost nine minutes, it looked as though the race and title were beyond reach. But with co-driver Peter Collins, Moss not only recovered that lost time but went on to win by nearly five minutes from the sister car of Fangio and Kling, and so clinch the title.

So Mercedes' two-year racing programme was completed just as it had started with a one-two victory. No name in the motor industry commanded greater respect, no emblem was more highly revered than the three-pointed star—the only decal carried by the great eights throughout their racing life. Mission was accomplished and the factory withdrew from racing.

Technical
excellence
1955-80

While Mercedes was whipping all comers on the track with the world's most advanced grand prix machinery in the mid-1950s, the company was producing a range of road cars that were superbly engineered and commercially very successful but hardly technical trendsetters. The base 180 saloon, for instance, still used an antiquated side-valve engine of basically pre-war design. D-B was not slow to capitalize on its racing reputation, however. The company's abrupt withdrawal from competition, which had absorbed a great deal of engineering time and talent, not to say a vast sum of money, was followed by the release of several new and revised production cars. Late in 1955 came the convertible version of the 220a with a shorter wheelbase than the saloon. Early in 1956 Mercedes announced the 220S with twin carburettors and 112 bhp, which demoted the old single-carb model to a 219, introducing another naming anomaly of the sort that has since made it difficult to keep track of the company's model line-up and numbering.

Model nomenclature

Immediately after the amalgamation of 1926, proper names—Stuttgart and Mannheim—were used to help cement the merger in the public eye. Since the early 1930s, however, D-B's model nomenclature has been based on a simple code. The numbers indicate the engine capacity and therefore the models' position in the range: 180 for 1.8 litres, 200 for 2 litres, 300 for 3 litres and so on. Following capital letters denote the type and character of the car: C for coupé, D for diesel, E (Einspritz) for fuel injection, L (Leicht) for lightweight, and K (Kurz) for short. So far so good. Since 1955, however, there have been many exceptions and additions to confuse the issue—or clarify it if you are familiar with the rules. The letter S, for example, which meant Sport in the 1950s (as in 300SLR or 3-litre Sport Light Racing—the R actually indicating *Rennwagen*, 'racing car'), stood loosely for Super as well in the '70s. Similarly, L could mean Lang (to indicate a long-wheelbase car) as well as Leicht (light). Small letters—a, b, c—were sometimes added to identify improved versions of existing models. The 220a was thus better in detail rather than concept than the 220 that preceded it. Later on, some models were to acquire suffix numbers, as in 450 SEL 6.9—in this case to indicate the presence of a 6.9-litre motor under the bonnet of a Super Einspritz Lang model normally powered by a 4.5-litre engine. Why not a 690SEL? Why not indeed? The absence of names or mark numbers, not to mention a styling policy of look-alike cars, has made an essentially straightforward product-planning programme, based on numerous variations of a few basic long-running engineering themes and body styles, seem more complex than it is.

All this may help to explain why the 180a of 1957 was not an improved 1.8-litre saloon as its name suggests but an economy low-compression version of the 190, introduced the year before with a detuned version of the 190SL's modern overhead-cam engine in the old rounded body of the original full-width 180. Updating existing bodyshells with new engines and running gear—and similarly equipping new body styles with existing mechanical components—is the key to Mercedes' evolutionary policy.

With the adoption of the 190 engine, the old side-valve unit, which had

PAGES 76/77 *Round-the-corner light cluster of a 1980 280SE, or 2.8-litre Super Einspritz (injection). The S-class cars were also made with larger V8 engines, including a lightweight 5-litre unit.*

LEFT *Mercedes' first full-width body, mounted on a pressed steel platform chassis that replaced the old oval-tube frame, was introduced in 1953 for the 180, successor to the 170. This 1958 version had an overhead valve engine in place of the original side-valve unit.*

ABOVE *No need for the controversial gullwing doors on the 1963 300SL soft-top roadster, one of the last to be made. A transverse compensating spring, linking the two rear swinging axles, improved handling.*

been in service for 20 years or so in one form or another, was at last dropped from the range. At the other end of the market spectrum a more powerful 250 bhp 300SL roadster lost its gullwing doors and gained a new version of the low-pivot rear suspension that was later to be adopted on lesser models, and the 220 was offered with semi-automatic Hydrak transmission. The column-mounted gear lever for the four-speed manual gearbox, mated to the engine through a fluid coupling, also acted as a touch-sensitive clutch control. The Hydrak did not last for very long. Fully automatic transmission of D-B's own design was to follow soon and oust the three-speed Borg-Warner self-change box used on the 300.

It was for the introduction of fuel injection, however, that Mercedes' mid-1950s passenger-car programme is perhaps best remembered. Developed in conjunction with Bosch, and perfected for use on the 300SL, 300SLR and W196 GP car, fuel injection soon filtered down the range. The 300 saloon and coupé were so equipped in 1955, increasing mid-range torque and top-end power by 1957 to 180 bhp, when a completely new injection system, squirting into the ports rather than the combustion chambers and sensitive to ambient temperature and atmospheric pressure, was standardized in a lengthened 300. The 130 bhp injected 220SE came the following year.

New body styles for the 1960s

By the late 1950s, with an ohc diesel 'four' in the base model—now well established for taxi use, but also popular with private and business buyers

for its economy and longevity—and high-performance injected sixes at the other end of the scale, Daimler-Benz had a fine line-up of modern powertrains but a somewhat dated range of body styles. That shortcoming was to a large extent answered by the introduction of a new 220 series at the 1959 Frankfurt show. Although the existing rounded bodies remained in production for the base cars until 1961, the 220 had completely new and elegant bodywork, longer, wider and lower than before. Flanking the traditional Mercedes grille were distinctive vertically stacked headlights contoured into wings that swept back to an angular tail treatment embracing vestigial fins. The 220 (105 bhp), 220S (124 bhp) and 220SE (130 bhp) all had this new, more roomy unitary body structure, as well as revised suspension. The geometry of the coil-and-wishbone set-up at the front was changed to give a higher roll centre, and short trailing-arm leaf springs provided additional fore and aft location. At the back, the single-joint, low-pivot swing-axle layout was further refined. The swinging arms enclosing the drive shafts retained their trailing locating links and coil-spring suspension, but were supplemented by a central transverse compensating coil spring, like that on the latest 300SL roadster, spanning the swing-axle pivot to increase bump stiffness but not resistance to roll. All this was a sophisticated ploy to help eradicate the inherent oversteer instability caused by the jacking effect of swinging axles under severe cornering and braking. Surprisingly, the new cars still had drum brakes, which were not replaced by discs (British-made Girling) until the 220SE Coupé and Convertible were announced in 1961.

The early 1960s range

It was not until the introduction that same year of the advanced 300SE—based on the 220's new bodyshell but with self-levelling air suspension, a limited-slip diff, all-disc (Dunlop) brakes operated by a hydraulic servo, D-B's own new four-speed automatic transmission and power steering—that the last of the tubular chassis-framed cars of pre-war ancestry was finally ousted from the range. The first postwar full-width body, introduced nearly a decade before for the 180, was also dropped around the same time, and the 190 petrol and diesel base models acquired the new square-cut look of the up-range cars, albeit with a simplified front-end treatment. D-B's policy of continuous overlapping improvement and updating was now in full swing, and reaping dividends in the market place.

Still the new shapes and models kept coming. The 230SL, faster and more luxurious than the 190SL it replaced, but less of an all-out sports car than the 300SL, was introduced at the 1963 Geneva show. In performance, price and character it was a brilliant compromise, though mechanically it owed far more to the 220SE saloon than to either of the superseded sportsters. If D-B had followed its labelling code to the letter, this Sport Light model should have been called the 230 SEL, for its 2306 cc engine, identical in stroke to the 220's but larger in bore, also had Bosch fuel injection of an improved six-plunger type. Power on a raised compression ratio of 9.3:1 was 170 bhp against the 220SE's 134, good enough to give a top speed of over 193 km/h (120 mph). This elegant, wide-tracked roadster, squatting on big 185 × 14 tyres made specially for it by Continental and Firestone, had disc/drum brakes, low-pivot swing-axle rear suspension with the new transverse compensating spring and, in closed form, a delectable slim-pillared hardtop with a distinctive concave roofline that later 250 and 280SL derivatives were to inherit.

Compared with D-B's range of the 1930s, only one model was now missing from the line-up: a super prestige saloon to equate with the great 7.7-litre Grosser Mercedes. That niche was filled in 1963 by the remarkable 600 twins—the 5/6-seater saloon and 7/8-seater Pullman limousine of almost railway-carriage proportions, a massive car outranking even the Rolls-Royce Phantom V in size and possibly in prestige too. Both models were endowed with a vigorous performance by a new 6.3-litre V8 engine that also powered a central hydraulic system which controlled the seats, chauffeur's division and windows, as well as the doors, bonnet,

80

ABOVE *Mercedes have excelled in many long-distance rallies like the 1979 Safari which Mikkola's 450SLC5.0 would have won but for hitting a bird.* INSET *Böhringer's 230SL rough-riding the Spa-Sofia-Liège marathon.*

RIGHT *The 230SL, introduced in 1963, was a compromise in performance, price and character between the superseded 190SL and 300SL.*

boot and dampers. Automatic transmission, power steering, self-levelling air-bag suspension and powered disc brakes were standard, though virtually anything that money could buy was available to special order by the car's tycoon and head-of-state customers.

Rally successes

Mercedes did not rest on its competition laurels after withdrawing from racing. With nothing more to prove on the track the company turned instead to rallying to demonstrate the speed and stamina of its road cars. The great German pairing of Walter Schock and Rolf Moll won the European championship in 1956 following victories in the tough Acropolis and Sestriere events driving a 300SL. They also surprised the pundits by finishing second in the Monte Carlo Rally with a 220 saloon, underlining that their fifth-place drive the previous year had been no fluke. Encouraged by this success, Mercedes embarked on an intensive rally programme that was probably to do more for the company's image and prestige than even the grand prix campaign had done, not least because it was conducted with big, heavy, luxury saloons that on paper were not ideally suited to tight special-stage events against the clock. That the cars' fabled strength and durability should carry them to several great trans-continental wins was perhaps less surprising, though no less creditable. Former GP ace, Karl Kling, now heading the competition effort, set Mercedes on the road to a now unrivalled marathon record by winning the Trans-Africa Rally, from Algiers to Cape Town, in a heavily laden 190 diesel. If that event across the Sahara did not make world news, the 1960 Monte Carlo Rally certainly did. The key to victory on the Monte, then at its zenith as the world's premier rally, was the final mountain circuit over which the team, under Kling's guidance, had practised for weeks beforehand in disguised cars, reminiscent of the way that Mercedes had tackled the 1914 French GP with painstaking care and preparation.

It paid off. Despite treacherous conditions the works 220SEs, introduced the previous year, finished first, second and third led by Schock and Moll. The same pair, certainly one of the greatest rally teams of all time, went on to score many other important successes, including a victory on the gruelling Acropolis which helped them gain the 1960 European rally championship. More big victories followed in 1961 for Mercedes cars, including wins on the Safari and the 4660 km (2900-mile) Argentinian Gran Premio, an all-out road race which the Schock/Moll 220SE won from the sister car of Herrmann/Gunzler against a strong field of over 200 starters. Again, it was meticulous preparation and practice that paved the way to victory in an event that Mercedes were to make their own private property.

Runner-up to Schock in the 1960 Monte had been a balding 37-year-old Stuttgart hotelier having his first drive for Mercedes. By 1962 Eugen Böhringer was not only leading the team but, along with Saab's Erik Carlsson, was the biggest name in rallying. He dominated many of the long-distance internationals, wins in the Acropolis and Liège–Sofia–Liège helping him towards the 1962 title, partnered for most of the time by Peter Lang, son of the former Mercedes grand prix driver. It was in 1962 that Ewy Rosqvist and Ursula Wirth beat all the men to win the Argentinian road race, an event that Böhringer was to win in 1963 and '64, on both occasions at the wheel of a 300SE, giving Mercedes four consecutive victories in what was probably the most gruelling motoring event in the world at the time.

The 230SL was also pressed into rally service, Böhringer winning the Spa–Sofia–Liège in one of the two-seater roadsters in 1963. Mercedes' rally ace was also brilliant on a racing track. Although beaten by two Lotus Cortinas into third place at Brands Hatch in *The Motor* six-hour race in 1964 (the first appearance of a works Mercedes in Britain since Moss's win at Aintree in the 1955 Grand Prix), he turned the tables on Ford a little later on the Nürburgring.

After all this intense competition activity, Daimler-Benz withdrew from all forms of rallying. Although Mercedes was to be represented by private entrants in some of the later big long-distance internationals, works-supported cars were not seen again until the 1977 London–Sydney Rally. Even then, it was largely a British initiative with factory assistance, though it

paid off handsomely: a pair of 280Es finished first (Andrew Cowan/Colin Malkin/Mike Broad) and second (Tony Fowkes/O'Gorman). The following year marathon masters Cowan and Malkin won the 30,000 km (18,650-mile) South American rally with a 450SLC in a full works onslaught that produced the familiar Mercedes first, second, third clean sweep. The prestigious Safari rally was also morally won by a Mercedes in 1979, Hannu Mikkola's 450SLC 5.0 being forced into second place after hitting a bird while leading.

The model changes, 1965–70, and the 'new generation'

Mercedes' prestige and reputation following its outstanding rally successes were never higher than when a bewilderingly comprehensive new range of graded models was introduced in 1965. The improved base cars, now 2-litre 200s in petrol and diesel form, retained the old fintail body style but the new middle and upper range 250/280/300 series, still with vertically encapsulated headlights, had improved running gear and new, low-waistline bodies with curved side windows and a crispness of line that was echoed, perhaps a little too closely, two years later in the much-vaunted 'new generation' cars for the 1968 season.

On the last-in, last-out principle, it was predictably the old fintailed body that was now ousted in a range change that affected every model in the line-up except the big 600s and sports cars. Everything else was subdivided into two groups. The more powerful cars—250S, 280S, 280SE (saloon, coupé and convertible) and 280SL (successor, through the 250SL, to the original 230SL)—were basically the same in appearance and design as the previous 250/300 series introduced three years earlier in 1965, though the 280 had a new, more powerful six-cylinder engine developing 140-170 bhp according to specification. It was the down-range cars—the 200/220 petrol and diesel fours and the 230/250 petrol sixes—that were most changed with their new bodies and suspension. The swinging rear axles, which had been progressively developed over a period of 30 years from a pre-war design, were replaced on the new generation of small models by a viceless semi-trailing independent layout, by now in wide use elsewhere, which virtually eliminated rear-wheel camber changes and any untoward oversteer or axle 'jacking' in the event of an emergency swerve. The swing-axle design had served Mercedes well but its shortcomings

1964 220SE coupe

ENGINE

Cylinders	Six in line, water-cooled
Bore/stroke mm	80 × 72.8
Capacity cc	2197
Valves	2 per cylinder, single chain-driven overhead camshaft
Compression ratio	8.7:1
Induction	Bosch fuel injection
Power	120 bhp (net) at 4800 rpm

DRIVE CHAIN

Clutch	Single dry plate or fluid coupling (automatic)
Gearbox	4-speed manual or 4-speed automatic in unit with engine
Drive	Propeller shaft to hypoid bevel final drive/diff unit

CHASSIS

Frame	Integral steel chassis and body unit
Front suspension	Independent by double wishbones and coil springs
Rear suspension	Independent single-joint low-pivot swing axles with coil springs and transverse compensating spring
Steering	Power-assisted recirculating ball
Brakes	Disc front, drum rear, with servo assistance and dual circuits
Wheels	Pressed steel disc
Weight	1410 kg (3108 lb)

PERFORMANCE

Max speed	177 km/h (110 mph)
Acceleration	0–60 mph 12 sec

Coupé
220 SE

were by now no longer really acceptable and they made Daimler-Benz a possible target for the American safety crusader Ralph Nader. Much was made at the time of the car's great strength (never really in question), and the active and passive safety features of the new-generation cars. The wide track, light steering, low noise levels and ergonomic switchgear were all emphasized as carefully researched and developed active safety measures. Impact-absorbing bodywork sandwiching a passenger 'safety cell', flush-fit door handles, interior crash padding, safety door locks, a collapsible steering column, protected fuel tank and so on were listed among the passive safety items.

The model line-up was soon expanded still further in 1968 with the exciting 300SEL 6.3. This astonishing luxury slingshot was the brainchild of development engineer and competition driver Erich Waxenberger. The story goes that Waxenberger, working on his own initiative, shoehorned the big V8 into an existing 300 bodyshell and then invited chief engineer Uhlenhaut to try the car without telling him what it was. Uhlenhaut set off in his usual press-on style and was amazed and mystified by the car's incredible performance. He lifted the bonnet at the first set of traffic lights to see what was beneath. That the car went into production is a tribute to

Waxenberger's foresight and initiative and to Uhlenhaut's forbearance with a staffman experimenting on the side. So formidable was the car's performance that a team of works 6.3s was entered for the Spa 24 hours saloon race. When it became obvious that breaking up of the tyres would mean failure—unthinkable to Mercedes—the cars were withdrawn after practice and little more was heard of them in competition, though Waxenberger himself won the Macau Grand Prix in one.

The following year, in 1969, a high-revving short-stroke single overhead camshaft 3.5-litre V8 was introduced as an alternative for the same saloon shell and new coupé and convertible versions of it.

PAGES 82/83 *The body style of this elegant 1964 220SE Coupé dates from 1961. A 120 bhp injected engine gave the car a lively performance.*

RIGHT *The 300 SEL of the mid 1960s had a six-cylinder engine of 3 litres; later models like this 1971 car were also available with 3.5- or 6.3-litre V8s.*

BELOW *The monster eight-seater 600 limousine, a prestige car for tycoons and heads of state, had a 6.3-litre V8 engine.*

The early 1970s

Some 50,000 230/250/280/SL roadsters had been made when the series was replaced in 1971 by the V8-engined open 350SL and 350SLC coupé, both with striking new wedge-shaped bodies and new-generation running gear, including semi-trailing rear suspension, leaving very little of the market spectrum uncovered from the 200/220 diesels (accounting for the bulk of base-car production) upwards. There were carburettor fours, normally aspirated and fuel-injected sixes from 2.3 to 2.8 litres, and injected V8s of 3.5 and 6.3 litres powering a range of saloon, coupé and convertible body styles. It was a line-up that no other manufacturer of quality cars in the world could match. Nor did it end there.

Two low-emission twin-cam 2.8-litre sixes—super-efficient engines capable of meeting America's stringent exhaust emission regulations—were introduced in 1972, one giving 160 bhp on carburettors, the other 185 bhp with Bosch fuel injection. First they powered new versions of the existing saloons and coupés. Later in 1972 they were to be used in the first models of a new up-market series of super saloons called the S-class, which Mercedes heralded as the closest reasonable approach to attainable perfection at an affordable price. Seven years' intensive research and development, in which the exciting experimental C111 Coupé (of which

ABOVE *The V8-engined 350SL and SLC, which replaced the 230/250/280SL series of six-cylinder cars, was introduced in 1971 and was still going strong at the turn of the decade, with six-cylinder engine and larger V8.*

RIGHT *A 1976 450SEL. The model number indicates the presence of a 4.5-litre V8 engine under the bonnet of a Super Einspritz Lang (long) saloon. The 450 series was acclaimed Car of the Year in 1973 by motoring journalists.*

more later) played a major part, went into the design of these big, luxurious cars, which replaced the previous generation of seven-year-old 280/300 models after some 350,000 had been made.

In shape, the solidly elegant S-class cars, still showing some family resemblance to the 'new generation' of small models—perhaps a little too much according to some critics—incorporated many detail design improvements affecting strength, safety, aerodynamics, comfort and refinement. The 'safety-cell' body, welded to a floorpan frame along now familiar lines, was immensely strong and carried new running gear, with double-wishbone suspension at the front incorporating zero offset steering, developed on the C111, to give run-straight stability even with, say, the inside wheel locked in the gutter under braking. At the back the old low-pivot swing axles, already replaced on the smaller cars, gave way to a fashionable semi-trailing layout. An improved version of Daimler-Benz's own power steering, which set the standard others were judged by according to contemporary road-test reports, was fitted, and there was a choice of transmissions: four-speed manual or automatic for the six-cylinder cars, and a new three-speed automatic for the 200 bhp V8-engined 350SE.

A 450 series of 4.5-litre V8s—acclaimed Car of the Year by an international jury of motoring journalists—supplemented the twin-cam 280 and 350 models in 1973, the long wheelbase version later spawning the redoubtable 225 km/h (140 mph) 6.9-litre 450SEL 6.9, a luxury slingshot that provided a combination of performance, comfort and

ABOVE *A 1978 long-wheelbase 240D. This quality car was no great performer but its running costs, particularly with a diesel engine, were very low. Down-range cars in the W123 series, introduced in 1976, were distinguished by their round headlights. More expensive models had rectangular units.*

RIGHT *Specialists had converted Mercedes saloons into estate cars for some years before Mercedes did the job itself in 1978. This is a 240TD (diesel) with built-in roofrack. T-cars also came with petrol engines.*

86

refinement to a degree that no other car in the world could match, with the possible exception of Jaguar's XJ12. Even-keel suspension that prevented nose dive under braking, and tail squat when accelerating hard, was a 450 refinement, though in most other respects the big V8s were much like the smaller S-class cars.

Much was made at the time of an anti-lock braking system that Mercedes had been developing for ages with Teldix, but production problems delayed its introduction as an expensive option for years.

Continuing development and research
Daimler-Benz by now led the world in diesel-car manufacture. The company had built over a million since the first 260D of 1936, and 1974 saw the production of nearly 150,000 diesel cars, which accounted for almost half D-B's output of passenger vehicles. Mercedes consolidated that position in 1974 by taking the diesel up-market with the introduction of a 3-litre 80 bhp five-cylinder saloon, confusingly called the 240D 3.0 to indicate that the unusual new engine powered one of the small-bodied cars. The demand for more economical luxury models in the wake of the first fuel crisis of the 1970s also prompted the introduction of 2.8-litre twin-cam versions of the sporting SL and SLC, hitherto powered only by 3.5- or 4.5-litre V8s. Such permutations have enabled Mercedes effectively to fill almost any emergent niche in its market spectrum with little delay, helped by computer-controlled production lines that have allowed considerable manufacturing flexibility.

Daimler-Benz has always been a big spender when it comes to ploughing back profits into the business. The company has invested vast sums not only in pure research and development for future generations of vehicles and systems but also in plant and advanced design and production techniques. Modern technology and traditional craftmanship go hand-in-hand at the Sindelfingen factory. For instance, in order to ensure the highest manufacturing standards, D-B spent 20 million Deutschmarks (£3.75 million at the time) on a pilot assembly line simply to study new production techniques, and also to train its polyglot workforce, for the next major car launch.

The late 1970s
By 1976 the 'new generation' of middleweight cars, now not so new after a production run of eight years and 1.8 million units, was replaced after a short period of overlap by the W123. Predictably, the new perceptibly wedge-shaped series, spanning the 200–280E range, resembled scaled-down S-cars and represented another evolutionary step forward rather than a revolutionary one. The top 280E model had rectangular head- and foglight nascelles to establish its position immediately below the similarly styled S-cars. Horizontally arranged circular headlights helped to identify the lesser models.

It was the cumulative influence of numerous detail improvements, many of them designed to meet new safety regulations, that made the W123 cars significantly superior to the models they replaced. They had stronger and slightly roomier bodies with rollcage protection from reinforced pillars and headrails; headlights that could be adjusted from inside the car; parallelogram wipers that swept more glass; a longer wheelbase to give greater passenger space; zero-offset steering and brake-pad wear indicators from the S-cars; a new safety column for the steering (power-assisted on all but the base 200 and 200D); better instruments; and simplified servicing aided by a diagnostic socket for plug-in electronic tuning. Engines and transmissions were carried over from the previous models, apart from a new 2.5-litre six with a four-bearing crank and nine counterbalance weights, and a new fuel-injection system—mechanical rather than electronic—for the 280E.

Coupés and the T-car estate—the first Mercedes had made, though specialist converters had produced them before from saloons—followed later; the estate was offered with a choice of five engines and self-levelling rear suspension to keep an even keel under load.

The 1979 G-range of four-wheel-drive all-purpose, all-terrain vehicles was another new departure, bridging the gap between the specialist Unimog and the new estates. Mercedes had announced in 1977 that a new factory was to be built at Graz, Austria, to manufacture the G-vehicles, developed in conjunction with Steyr-Daimler-Puch. With a choice of three engines of four, five or six cylinders—the only major units to be used from the car range—three body styles and two different wheelbases, there was a total of 40 variations on the basic G-car theme, all based on a strong box-section chassis frame. One of the most notable of many unusual design features was the use of total differential locks on either or both of the live axles, so that even if only one wheel was in

A 450SLC registered in 1980. This is the fixed head coupé version. Open and closed cars were also made with the 2.8-litre twin-cam six-cylinder engine (named the 280SL) and a 240 bhp 5-litre light-alloy V8 known less logically as the 450SLC 5.0.

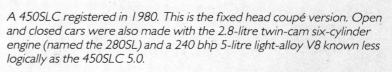

contact with the ground, progress could still be maintained.

Daimler-Benz also joined the growing ranks of turbo manufacturers in 1979, not with a high-performance petrol engine but with a blown 300SD diesel unit in a W123 body, manufactured with the economy and emission-conscious North American market in mind. Technical director Hans Scherenberg confirmed that the new turbo, which in 200 bhp form had powered a special C111 Coupé to several international speed records the year before, was part of a vigorous programme of diesel-car development. Some years previously Mercedes had predicted that pending emission and fuel-consumption legislation in the United States would make the diesel, particularly in turbocharged form, very attractive. Petrol engines, the company forecast, would become increasingly more difficult and expensive to make in order to satisfy the new clean-air and miles-per-gallon laws, while the cost of the diesel, inherently 'cleaner' (despite its black exhaust smoke) and more economical, would remain much the same. The introduction by General Motors of a Cadillac, no less, with a diesel V8 in 1979 underlines just how right the Daimler-Benz concern was to put its faith and a great deal of money into the diesel. In the wake of the second—and permanent—fuel crisis of the late 1970s, the introduction of the 300SD could hardly have been better timed.

A new all-alloy 5-litre petrol V8 announced at the same time, although lighter and more efficient than the elderly iron-block 4.5- and 6.9-litre engines it was designed to replace, may have a less certain future. It was first used, almost as a trial run, in the 450SLC. The car it was primarily intended for, though, was the new S-class, announced in the autumn of 1979. The shape was unmistakably Mercedes, but it was sufficiently different and striking to answer previous criticisms that the most expensive cars had not been distinctive enough, not sufficiently different from the cheaper models.

Such a complaint could not be levelled at the latest, superbly proportioned flagship, designed for a production run that could well span the 1980s. The narrower body, strongly tapered front to rear, was distinctly shovel-nosed and wedge-shaped in profile, resulting in a 14 per cent reduction in drag compared with the previous cars. Slightly less weight also helped to reduce the fuel-guzzling tendencies of a car that, in a worsening fuel crisis, could yet finish up as a diesel. The new S models were announced, however, with a rationalized range of petrol engines in normal and long-wheelbase forms (and no anomalies in the nomenclature either): 280S, 280SE/SEL, 380SE/SEL and 500SE/SEL, the 380 being a smaller version of the new 5-litre alloy V8 rather than an enlarged 350.

A longer wheelbase gave more room for passengers at the small expense of luggage accommodation (still generous) in the new short-tail boot. There were also new seats, larger doors, regrouped switchgear, more wood trim to highlight the plush appointments, automatic heater controls, less noise and incredible attention to detail. Hydropneumatic suspension and anti-lock brakes—now ready for production after a decade's development so high are Mercedes' standards—were promised as future options.

The continuing energy problem casts a shadow over the future of such big, fast, fuel-greedy cars, but with a growing range of refined and economical diesels Mercedes, at the time of writing, is better placed than most manufacturers to meet an uncertain future. Not until the late 1970s was the true value of the decision taken nearly half a century before—to continue development of Karl Benz's diesels—fully appreciated.

1980 280SE			
ENGINE		**CHASSIS**	
Cylinders	Six in line, water-cooled	Frame	Unitary body/chassis unit
Bore/stroke mm	86 × 78.8		
Capacity cc	2746	Front suspension	Independent by coil springs and wishbones
Valves	2 per cylinder, twin overhead camshafts	Rear suspension	Independent by semi-trailing arms and coil springs
Compression ratio	9:1		
Induction	Bosch mechanical fuel injection	Steering	Power-assisted recirculating ball
Power	185 bhp at 5800 rpm		
		Brakes	Servo-assisted dual-circuit discs front and rear
DRIVE TRAIN			
Clutch	Single dry plate or torque converter	Wheels	Pressed steel
Gearbox	4-speed manual or automatic	Weight	1562 kg (3440 lb)
Drive	Propeller shaft to hypoid bevel differential assembly	**PERFORMANCE**	
		Max speed	211 km/h (131 mph)
		Acceleration	0–60 mph 9.3 sec.

Latest of a long line of super saloons produced by Mercedes. This is the 280SE 'six': at the top end of the range comes the all-alloy 5-litre V8. INSET *The luxurious interior of the 280SE.*

Three-pointed stars

Whether for company prestige, as German propaganda or for plain product improvement, Daimler-Benz has produced many outstanding 'specials' in its long history. Earlier chapters have touched on the great racing cars, but some of the record breakers and experimental prototypes have been no less remarkable in their way.

The T80: a bid for the ultimate record

Grand prix-based streamliners pushed a number of international Class B (5 to 8 litre) records to nearly 433 km/h (269 mph) in the late 1930s. But Germany also wanted to wrest the ultimate prize, the world land speed record, from Britain's grip too, and for that Daimler-Benz had to aim very high indeed. Malcolm Campbell's *Bluebird* had exceeded 480 km/h (300 mph) for the first time in September 1935. George Eyston's mighty *Thunderbolt* raised the record to 502 km/h (312 mph) two years later, and to over 555 km/h (345 mph) in 1938. John Cobb was the first man to exceed 563 km/h (350 mph) but his Railton record lasted for only 24 hours. The following day Eyston replied with 574 km/h (357 mph) on the same Bonneville Salt Flat strip. In 1939 Cobb cracked it again at 592 km/h (367.7 mph) and it was this record that Daimler-Benz had to beat with the remarkable Porsche-designed T80 monster.

Sheer brute power was the key to such enormous speeds, and like Campbell, Eyston and Cobb, Dr Porsche turned to a colossal aero engine to provide it. Daimler-Benz's 44.5-litre supercharged V12 603 was normally rated at 1750 bhp but, for the short duration of an LSR run, it could no doubt have been tuned to give nearer 3000 bhp. Porsche resolved the problem of traction by transmitting the drive through a gearless fluid coupling to four large wire-spoked rear wheels—two pairs in tandem—just behind the mid-mounted inverted engine, ahead of which sat the driver. The chassis, made of massive oval-section steel tubes, was clothed by a long, low, slender all-enveloping body carried on outriggers from the chassis and supported by a lightweight tubular skeleton frame. Huge side aerofoil fins were designed to increase stability and downforce on the powered wheels at high speed in much the same way that racing cars were later to depend heavily on upside-down 'wings'.

The T80, which was to have been driven by Hans Stuck of Auto Union fame and not, surprisingly, by Mercedes' Caracciola, was designed for well over 640 km/h (400 mph) and would no doubt have achieved such a speed but for the outbreak of war, which foiled the record attempt.

The Wankel-engined C111

In 1961 Daimler-Benz acquired the licence from the patent holders NSU to manufacture and sell the rotary Wankel engine, brainchild of Dr Felix Wankel, provided it was petrol powered and developed over 50 bhp. By 1966 two- and three-rotor engines were ready for passenger-car evaluation and, by the late 1960s, Daimler-Benz was probably as far advanced as anyone in Wankel development even though not producing rotaries for sale. In the light of the catastrophic problems encountered by NSU's Ro80—a superb car powered by a prematurely released twin-rotor engine with so short a life that it crippled its makers with warranty claims—the company was probably wise to keep its Wankel to itself and merely demonstrate its remarkable qualities to the press.

It was partly for this reason that the C111 Coupé was built, though the car was to serve several other purposes too. Mercedes had not built a real racing car since the W196 of 1955 and, although the C111 was never to be used in competition, it was designed along modern mid-engined racing-car lines. In short, D-B was keeping its hand in with an exciting flag-waving testbed that would also be a useful experimental tool.

It was first shown in public at the 1969 Frankfurt show. Its low-drag wedge-shaped glassfibre body was bonded and riveted to a fabricated sheet-steel platform chassis that carried a 141 kg (310 lb) three-rotor Wankel engine developing 280 bhp at 7000 rpm from 3.6 litres. The power/weight ratio advantage over the 200 bhp 3.5-litre V8, which weighed 225 kg (495 lb), was clearly evident, and its turbine smoothness a revelation. In 1972 Mercedes released a second generation C111/2 with a four-rotor engine of 4.8-litre displacement developing 350 bhp. This car could accelerate from rest to 97 km/h (60 mph) in 4.8 seconds, and do over 300 km/h (187 mph), but it was the smoothness of its engine, its remarkable roadholding and the effectiveness of its experimental anti-lock brakes that most impressed the few lucky outsiders who were privileged to drive it. By now it was clear that Mercedes had no intention of racing the C111—it would have been no match for the all-conquering Porsche 917 that was then upholding German racing prestige—or even to sell it as a roadgoing supercar to a few rich and discerning customers. It served its time well, though, as a promotional vehicle as well as a research and

development testbed: it was used to develop the S-class cars' zero-offset steering and front suspension and ABS anti-lock braking system.

Although D-B was to resolve the *mechanical* problems associated with the Wankel—notably rapid rotor-tip and housing wear—heavy fuel consumption, poor low-speed torque and, above all, a 'dirty' exhaust eventually caused Mercedes to shelve the rotary programme. Only Toyo Kogyo, makers of Mazda cars in Japan, persevered with it on a commercial scale despite a crippling sales crisis after the 1973 fuel scare when demand for their thirsty rotaries dwindled overnight on the American market.

In 1973 the only working C111/2 left from the 1970 series was brought out of retirement as a record breaker, not with Wankel power this time but with a turbocharged five-cylinder diesel, the engine on which Daimler-Benz was now pinning its hopes to beat America's emission and fuel-consumption legislation. With its Garret turbocharger spinning to 135,000 rpm, the 2999 cc engine (it had slightly narrower bores than standard to bring the capacity within the 3-litre limit) developed 190 bhp at 4500 rpm, sufficient to capture 16 international speed records previously held by petrol-powered cars, most of them by a Porsche 911. On Fiat's 12.656 km (7.8-mile) banked circular track at their Narda proving grounds in southern Italy, the well-worn diesel C111 covered 16,100 km (10,000 miles) at an average speed of over 253 km/h (157 mph) breaking Ab Jenkins' 40-year-old 5000-mile mark of 240 km/h (149 mph) on the way. In 64 hours of flat-out motoring by four of D-B's drivers, the car averaged 19.8 litres per 100 km (14.3 mpg).

journalist Paul Frère, one of the four drivers, recalled in *Motor* how he clinched a number of absolute world records up to 500 km only to have them fractionally bettered a few hours later when the first run was aborted following a thrown tyre tread which damaged the body. Dr Hans Liebold, the development engineer in charge of the C111 project, restarted the run in the marginally quicker spare car (who but Mercedes would have built two?) and deprived Frère of the records he had just set. The second run was also later delayed, and stopped at the 12-hour mark after averaging 314 km/h (195.4 mph) following an encounter with a luckless hedgehog that damaged the front spoiler. Even so, the car broke nine absolute world records for any class of car or engine, including putting a tantalizing 321.843 km (199.984 miles) into the first hour. Perhaps even more amazing is that the fuel consumption at 322 km/h (200 mph) was over 16.6 litres per 100 km (17 mpg), demonstrating what could be achieved with good streamlining, very long-legged gearing and a high thermal efficiency. It was a lesson that would not be soon forgotten.

Towards safer cars

Not all Daimler-Benz's experimental cars have been concerned with speed of course. Many of the special features embodied in the 1972 ESV (Experimental Safety Vehicle) were later to find their way into production models. Based on a 250 shell with modified 350SL running gear, the ESV was designed to protect its occupants from injury in an 80 km/h (50 mph) impact, front or rear. Its massive rubber-faced bumpers were carried on hidden hydraulic rams within an 'eggbox' structure designed to absorb the concentrated penetration of, say, a lamp post or telegraph pole. So space-consuming were these crush zones that there was room under the bonnet for only threequarters of the normal V8: in other words a 2778 cc V6. With so much extra weight and less power, performance and economy were not strong points of the ESV. Rubber facing on the doors and mirrors was for the protection of pedestrians but it was for the car's occupants that most concern and ingenuity were shown. Closing the burst-proof doors triggered into position an automatic seat harness designed to restrain its wearer in a 48 km/h (30 mph) collision; air bags handled more severe impacts. The interior was heavily padded, the lights and windows kept clear with five wipers, and the brakes naturally incorporated the ABS anti-lock system. It was all very impressive but prohibitively expensive as a production car. Moreover the growing demand for material and fuel conservation was not compatible with such energy-heavy safety tanks. As a tangible demonstration of Mercedes' concern for safety, not to say a data-collecting tool for future production vehicles, Mercedes' ESV served its purpose well, especially as it was based on a production shell.

Reporting on the company's operations in the 1970s, Mercedes observed that 'anyone who has a very good name has to work extremely hard to keep it. He must never ease up, never make a big mistake, and anything which is new must always be better. Always. The only thing that is surprising is that people still envy us . . .'

Envy? Is not the word respect?

PAGES 92/93 AND LEFT *The C111 experimental car in three stages of development. Most were Wankel-powered but later record-breakers used diesel engines.*

ABOVE *The 1939 T80 Land Speed Record car, designed for over 640 km/h (400 mph).*

BELOW *Mercedes' Experimental Safety Vehicle (ESV) of 1972.*

The C111/3 turbo car

Capitalizing on the new performance image it had created for the diesel, the company introduced its 300SD turbo in America the following year. The record breaking did not end there, though. It was obvious that much higher speeds could be attained with a purpose-built streamlined body and only a small increase in power. The experimental department's C111/3 not only had a longer wheelbase and a narrower track to cut down on frontal area, but a tailfinned body with an astonishingly low drag factor. By increasing the turbo boost to 30 psi, the 3-litre diesel's output was raised to 235 bhp at 4500 rpm, which was enough to push the car's top speed to over 320 km/h (200 mph). Former GP driver and motoring

Index

References to illustrations are in italics

Acknowledgements

The publishers would like to thank the following individuals and organizations for their kind permission to reproduce the photographs in this book:

Geoffrey Goddard 27, 31 left and right, 34–35, 52–53 below, 75 below; LAT 6–7; Mercedes-Benz (UK) Ltd 55 below, 92–93, 94–95 above; George Monkhouse 50–51, 73 above; Peter Roberts 11 above, 13 above, 16 above, 21, 26 above, 53 above, 56–57 above, 72–73 below, 80 inset; Colin Taylor 80.

Special photography by:

Rainer Schlegelmilch Endpapers, 1, 2–3, 4–5, 8–9, 10, 11 below–12 below, 13 below–15, 16 below–19, 22–25, 26 below, 28–30, 32–33, 35 below–37, 40–41, 49 below, 54–55, 57 below–59, 62 above–65, 68–71, 74–75 above, 76–77, 90–91, 94 below.

Andrew Morland 20, 38, 39 above, 48 above–49 above, 60–61, 66–67, 78 below–79 above, 81–83, 86, 86–87 below.

Laurie J. Caddell 39 centre and below, 84–85, 87 above, 88–89.

The publishers would also like to thank the Daimler-Benz Museum in Germany for making available most of the cars that appear in this book. In addition, thanks are due to the following owners for allowing their cars to be photographed:

W. Allen 49 top, 60–61; Brian Classic Ltd 39 centre and below; Coys of Kensington 39 top; Ron Cushway 79; Daimler-Benz AG 76–77, 90–91; Richard Grey 48 below; C.W.P. Hampton 38 below; Anne Mercedes Honour 48 top; John de Grave Cars 85; J. Lightfoot 20; R.D. Lloyd 82–83; Mercedes-Benz (UK) Ltd 86–87, 88–89; B. Naylor 78; Peter Parsons 67 top; David Prior 81; J.A. Slade 66–67; John Turner, Bruton's of London 84–85.